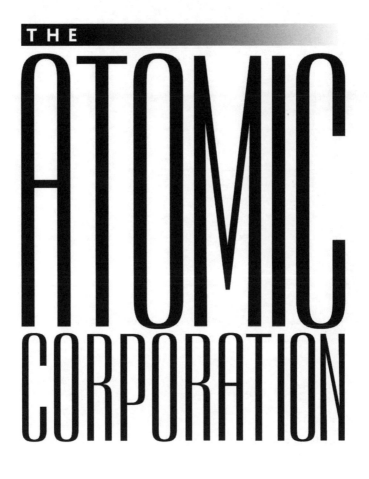

WITH A FOREWORD BY **CHRIS MEYER,** AUTHOR OF ***BLUR*** & ***FUTURE WEALTH***

THE ATOMIC CORPORATION

A RATIONAL PROPOSAL FOR UNCERTAIN TIMES

ROGER CAMRASS  MARTIN FARNCOMBE

CAPSTONE

First published 2001 by
Capstone Publishing Limited (a Wiley company)
8 Newtec Place
Magdalen Road
Oxford OX4 1RE
United Kingdom
http://www.capstone.co.uk

British Library Cataloguing in Publication Data
A CIP catalogue record for this book is available from the British Library

ISBN 1-84112-172-X

Typeset in 11/16 pt Bodoni Book by
Sparks Computer Solutions Ltd, Oxford
http://www.sparks.co.uk
Printed and bound by
T.J. International Ltd, Padstow, Cornwall

This book is printed on acid-free paper

Substantial discounts on bulk quantities of Capstone books are available to corporations,
professional associations and other organisations. For details telephone Capstone Publishing on
(+44-1865-798623), fax (+44-1865-240941) or email (info@wiley-capstone.co.uk).

Contents

Foreword by Christopher Meyer   vii

Preface and Acknowledgements   xi

PART I: DEPARTURE   1

1   Welcome to the Atomic Corporation   3

PART II: DISCONTINUITIES   21

2   Land of the Giants   23
3   Towards a New-World Context   38
4   A Revolution in Digital Connectivity   50

PART III: DRIVERS   61

5   New Sources of Shareholder Wealth   63
6   Relational Capital   78

PART IV: DESTINATION   93

7   Let's Meet the Atoms   95
8   Making the Molecules Work   113
9   Atomizing the Corporation   127
10   Atomic Numbers   144
11   Industrial (R)evolution   158
12   New Partnerships, New Wealth   178

PART V: DESTINY   197

13   The Atomized Individual   199

Notes   207
Glossary   213
Index   217

Foreword

"ECONOMY" IS THE NAME WE GIVE to the process of using our resources to fulfil our desires. Our economies have demanded resources throughout history but the way they have used them has changed with the rhythm of technological and environmental progress. For the past hundred years or so, the fastest growing economies have chosen to organize themselves into corporations as the most efficient means of production. And since most of us reading this book have grown up in that context, it's easy for us to think it will always be so, just as feudal serfs, guild members, and farmers did in their respective times. The technologies that have transformed value creation will likewise revolutionize economic organization; shifting power from institutions to the talent they rely on.

The most important innovation of the industrial revolution was not a technology like the Bessemer steel-making process or the Newcomen steam engine, it was the legal creation of limited liability enterprises – corporations. Why? Because it mobilized the flow of capital, which was a scarce and illiquid resource in the late 19th century. A blacksmith might start a business based on his family's savings, or what could be borrowed from the village he would serve. But Andrew Carnegie needed financial capital on a different scale and it's no accident that his name is connected to that of Paul Mellon, the founder of the bank that funded U.S. Steel. The growth of the banking system and the ability to fund industrial-scale projects were enabled by the development of the corporate form of organization.

The power of this new economic species proved almost too great. The industrial technologies that corporations developed on a mass scale – like chemistry, electricity, or mass production – created so much value and required so much capital that they eventually acquired enormous leverage. In fact, they accumulated power so rapidly that democratic societies had to create new institutions to curb them – first the anti-Trust laws, then the Labour Movement and associated legal framework. Most recently, it has been consumerism that has again reduced the corporations' room for maneuver. Even so, the corporation seems to be gaining ground as global enterprises take on capabilities that used to belong to governments. Few central banks, for example, can compete with Citicorp in currency markets. What could change this picture of growing corporate dominance?

Over the past five years, the traditional corporation got a bit of a *frisson* from the dot.com boom. Right now, of course, that fear has become a sneer as Aeron chairs – the emblematic furniture of Silicon Valley – can be picked up for next to nothing at auctions and individual "free agency" looks more scary than liberating. But this does not mean the corporation is safe.

Clayton Christensen[1] has recently driven home a forceful point: when a technology with truly disruptive potential first emerges, it doesn't work very well. It gets used only in niches where its specific advantages are strongest. The existing technology is generally too well developed in the better established applications to give way to the interloper in its early, crude state. Thus, transistors were first popularized in tinny radios because, without the transistor's low weight and power consumption a portable radio wasn't possible at all – never mind that the radio sounded horrible.

But the new technology learns from its niche, improves, and pretty soon names like DuMont, RCA, Philco, and the other vacuum-tube dependent companies have disappeared. Christensen's conclusion is this: successful corporations are generally managed according to the sort of rules that militate against investing in new and risky technology.

The foregoing argument relates to product technologies, but it applies equally to new forms of organization. The dot.com economy, made of small companies and free agents, bound together by their shared mastery of new networking technology and an equally shared set of values about knowledge, relationships, and competition, invented an economy perfect for the rapid proliferation of information-based, non-capital-intensive businesses – the early niche. The collapse of many of these businesses has not wiped out this way of working, only the recent approach to getting such companies funded – and the experiences of the dot.com cohort will lead to even more startling organizational innovation, as the transistor led to the microprocessor.

The connected and fluid labor markets that bred the dot.coms still exist, just as Internet-based communication still exists among the Chinese intelligentsia even after Tiananmen Square. And this is the disruptive technology that will eventually weaken the corporation. The corporation's last remaining monopoly power (in theory – we'll await the result of the Microsoft trial) is created by the inefficiency of the labor market, which keeps individuals from seeking new jobs as easily as they do new cars. The Net is changing this rapidly, to the benefit of the most talented individuals. As Charles Handy says, "the big challenge for the elephants is that they don't end up as the home for the second rate."

The corporation as we know it is, in fact, in trouble. There is nothing to prevent its demise now that what had previously been its advantages become less important. In fact, its accumulation of power will come to be seen as a kind of historical aberration, like centrally planned economies. This is a big story for the next decade and it should already be capturing our attention. The technologies of communication and collaboration will drive economic power from the institution to the individual, and the decisions about how our resources fulfill our desires will be revolutionized.

How?

Roger Camrass and Martin Farncombe have done a courageous thing, and the right one: they have broken the corporation into its constituent elements, identified the forces that determine how these elements can and will be put back together, and predicted the combinations that will thrive over the next ten years. Rather than picking this or that trend, declaring it universal, and extrapolating it, they have created a chemistry of enterprise, allowing chemical engineers all over the economy to start making their own new compounds, testing them, and determining those that are the most promising. And they have got the crucial drivers absolutely right: connectivity replacing many of the advantages of scale; financial capital giving way to human and intellectual capital; the emergence of new types of entities. But above all, they have signaled a critical change in perspective, from an economy of monolithic and self-contained institutions looking at life from the top down, to a network of atomic entities constantly forming new relationships and creating value from the bottom up.

In *The Atomic Corporation*, they lay out both the periodic table of elements and rules for this chemistry, and describe some of the new things that can be fashioned with it. No doubt, many more things will be created than anyone can foresee. But the process is essential: deconstruct the ways that value is added in corporations today, examine the forces that will alter this picture, and analyze the components that will support value creation in the future.

This networked, bottom-up perspective parallels powerful currents in today's economy – like individual-based data mining and mass customization – as well as tomorrow's, with the focus on value created at the molecular level through biotechnology, nanotechnology, and advances in materials. The bottom-up view will prevail, and will upend our views of resource management. Corporate power, and its pathological cousin, the influence of financial analysts, will be eroded. As we find new ways to organize around our desires – including how we want to work and manage our own professional lives – we will create the kind of economic chemistry that Camrass and Farncombe describe. In the process, an economy of the people, by the people, and for the people may reappear.

The corporation looks to be in full cry, with corporate executives not only highly paid but lionized – Jack Welch got an $8 million book advance. But their bubble will burst as surely as it did for the dot.coms and, if corporations are to extract value from the assets they have built they must understand the source of the power of the insurgents and the forms the alternatives may take. *The Atomic Corporation* is a guide to transforming the value locked within the corporation into a new form, adapted to the connected economy and able to continue adapting on its own. It illustrates a challenge that will face every corporate leader in the decade to come.

Christopher Meyer
Director, Center for Business Innovation
Cap Gemini Ernst & Young
Cambridge, MA

Preface and Acknowledgements

THE WRITING OF THIS BOOK may have been compressed into a six-month period but the journey that led its two authors to their conclusions started more than a quarter of a century ago. It began back in 1974, the year the world's first microprocessor was manufactured, the moment identified by the Intel Museum in California as the dawn of the digital age. Since then, digital technology has sent wave after wave of change crashing over the business world. Our book concentrates on four specific manifestations of this digitally-inspired change. The first was the digitization of global telecommunications networks in the seventies. This was followed by the democratization of computing with the advent of the PC in the eighties. Thereafter came the transformation of corporate enterprises through business re-engineering and process re-design in the nineties, and most recently, the universal adoption of the global Internet and World Wide Web.

This remarkable succession of events left no corner of business untouched. Working patterns, our social environment, and political agendas have all been turned upside down by the increasing power and influence of a connected economy. And from the relative industrial and social stability of the early seventies, the world has become progressively more chaotic and unpredictable. Now we have reached the point where people crave a new sense of purpose and direction.

So how did we reach the Atomic Corporation? Towards the end of 2000, we saw a dramatic rise in the numbers of new marketplaces spawned by large corporations. We both knew that these marketplaces, if they were to work at all, would erode the boundaries of the corporations. We found ourselves idly discussing what we thought might happen if this erosion were taken to its limits, and as we started to look at the economic and social forces shaping the economy, we realized that they were all driving corporations towards atomization. As winter drew in, we started to look in more detail at the creation and viability of an economy made of these atoms. The final step was discovering the concept of relational capital, the idea that this epic restructuring would release previously unexploited value embedded in all the corporation's relations with external parties. It was this realization that turned atomization from a possible destination for corporations into a desirable and probably inevitable direction. *The Atomic Corporation* was born.

But to present a comprehensive snapshot of today's digital revolution, and to be bold enough to ascribe some order within the ensuing chaos, requires more than a mere point of view. It calls for credible research and experience that goes well beyond the combined authority of just two individuals. In this respect, we are indebted to several institutions through which we have gained personal access to the knowledge and collective wisdom that provides reliable commentary on today's profound events. We acknowledge gratefully the following people and organizations that have contributed the intellectual underpinnings to this book.

The Center for Business Innovation in Cambridge, Massachusetts, and the associated work of its director, Chris Meyer and his colleague Stan Davies, have contributed much to our understanding both of the connected economy and the underlying financial metrics that determine corporate success in this new era. Their ongoing Innovation Program and research into "Measures that Matter" have been particularly helpful in this respect.

From a practical viewpoint, the recent forum to examine the formation of a global horizontal marketplace – the Internet Services Venture Vehicle – convened by Cap Gemini Ernst & Young in 2000, has helped greatly to expand our thinking on global partnerships. This initiative was supported by 12 of the world's leading companies. We thank the senior executives of these organizations whose personal contributions have led to a new vision of the collective enterprise. Named here are Dan Mauer of Procter & Gamble, Rand Barbarno of Hewlett-Packard, Jo Gibbs of BP Amoco, Michael Lap of Morgan Stanley Dean Witter and Jackson Cosey of The Coca-Cola Company.

Two other influential studies of the future have provided detailed research and evidence for our findings. "Business in the Third Millennium," undertaken from 1992–1998, was managed by SRI International and subsequently by FirstMatter LLC on behalf of ten global sponsors. These included companies such as Chevron, EPRI, GRI and the US Postal Service in the USA; BP, ICL and Barclays in the UK; and NTT and Fujitsu in Japan. This study examined the impact of new information infrastructures such as the Internet on relationships between industry, government and the individual. Thanks goes to Gill Ringland of Fujitsu ICL who initiated the study, Cornellia Varney and Allen Phipps of SRI who provided much of the program and commercial management, and Watts Wacker, SRI's Resident Futurist and co-founder of First-Matter for his thought leadership. Secondly, "Management in the Nineties," undertaken by the Massachusetts Institute of Technology on behalf of 12 industrial sponsors, which was the direct predecessor of Business in the Third Millennium. This program led to the development of business re-engineering and business process redesign that was commercialized by consulting firms such as CSC Index and Gemini Consulting in the early nineties.

The authors acknowledge the particular work of colleagues such as Jim Champy, Mike Hammer, Ron Chrisman and Fred Wiersema of CSC Index in the intellectual development of corporate atomization, and more recently the parallel development of thinking from Mainspring Consulting on the atomization of the telecoms industry.

Prior to these two programs, Roger was intimately involved in one of the world's leading CIO programs – the Butler Cox Foundation – that undertook extensive research on behalf of over 500 major corporations across Europe. Projects covering every aspect of information technology, from database design and distributed processing to IS efficiency and effectiveness, were meticulously chartered through the seventies and eighties on behalf of the member organizations. The Foundation became one of Europe's leading IT forums and is fondly remembered by its charter members. Thanks go to George Cox, David Eggleton, David Butler and Roger Woolfe who invested their personal time and effort to make this forum a success.

And beyond these major programs, it is important to mention the many partners and colleagues of Cap Gemini Ernst & Young who have provided tireless support and intellectual input into our thinking. Few organizations could have been more supportive to new and provocative ideas – reflecting the innovative flavor of CGEY's culture across the globe. The list of valuable contributors is too long for this book, but we mention a few special friends and collaborators – Brendan Mullany, Malcolm McKenzie and Andy Mulholland for their perspectives on e-business; and Sam Dunnachie, Paul Thorley and Richard Seurat for their executive support of the Atomic Corporation project. In particular, we would like to recognize the contribution of Emily-Claire Hutchinson and David Fox with research and production.

We are also grateful for the help and encouragement of Phil Deane and Mike Jacobs at A.T. Kearney, to our publisher, Mark Allin of Capstone-Wiley for being an instant believer, and to our literary agent, Rafe Sagalyn of the Sagalyn Agency, for his commercial skills and international perspectives. Our editor, Chris Davison, smoothed off many of the rough edges, and while Susi Camrass helped spread the word about atomization amongst the business community, Judy Farncombe brought atoms to the Web. Without these contributions, we could not have made this book a success.

Finally, we could not have produced this work without the active support of our wives and families. Thank you, ladies, and sorry about the vacations.

PART I
Departure

Bill Gates was right – the Internet *did* change everything – but perhaps not in the way that Bill was anticipating. Did he foresee corporations scrabbling to get smaller, competitors sharing assets and staff, middle managers becoming CEOs of billion dollar spin-offs?

Looking at the developments of today we think these will be the news headlines of tomorrow. Welcome to the new theory of the firm. Welcome to the Atomic Corporation.

CHAPTER 1

Welcome to the
Atomic Corporation

O UR BOOK IS ABOUT THE RADICAL CHANGES that are going to sweep across the
global economy in the next decade. It is about the seismic impact these
changes will have on today's big corporations, the way they will break up under
pressure, and the evolution of a new landscape populated by much smaller
business units.

We call these units "atoms." We will describe how and why they will be
small, specialist and very agile. Then we will explain how these new corporate
"atoms" will bind together to form "molecules," the future means of delivering
more accurately and efficiently the demands of tomorrow's customers. They
will mark the end of today's oversized, introspective, and often unresponsive
corporations.

It is a dramatic thesis. We predict, for example, that typical atoms will
have payrolls closer to 100 people than 100,000. The implications for us all,
as consumers, employees or managers, will be enormous. We will have to learn
new skills, become correspondingly more adaptable in this New World, and
may very well end up working portfolio careers rather than experiencing life-
long employment.

Atoms will concentrate on one specialty from a basket of business competencies – chief among which will be product innovation, process excellence,
asset management, customer relationships, and value networking.

The speed of change and the new demands of our business future will
be unforgiving. Hence the centrality of these new atoms to the survival and
success of corporations. They are the shape of winning businesses in the connected economy. And freed from the constraints of size, the atoms will be able
to adapt to ever-changing circumstances, and the demands of a much more
powerful consumer. In this New World, value will be delivered to consumers

not through the corporation but through a complex and ever changing web of business-to-business connections – what we call the molecule.

Welcome to the new theory of the firm – the Atomic Corporation.

THE END OF CORPORATE EMPIRES

We can see already where this force of change is coming from in the world around us today. Changes in customer expectations, changes in the cost of doing business, and changes in stock market valuations are commonplace. They are the subject of books, magazines, television documentaries and our own experience. None of them is in itself capable of turning our business world upside down but in combination they are enough to tear apart even the biggest of our giant corporations. At the heart of it all lies a single phenomenon – an emerging information infrastructure that alters dramatically the costs of co-ordination and dispersion of knowledge. This is the real consequence of the Internet revolution.

The changing customer

Consumers and business customers are already familiar with using electronic portals on the Internet to compare price and diversity of goods and services from thousands of suppliers across the world. They have been empowered by this technological progress. But each individual interaction also gives suppliers unique marketing data and insight into the personal preferences of each individual, which helps restore some of the balance in the shifting relationship.

In just a quarter of a century, we have witnessed the introduction of over six billion silicon devices into our daily lives – one for every member of the human race, with every prospect of a trillion interconnected entities by the end of the coming decade.

We have already seen the location and ownership of information changing in our lifetimes as this number has grown. In the 1960s, information about "me" belonged to "them" – the data high priests who controlled the mainframe computers. The personal computer helped change that by democratizing the power of the technology – putting it within everybody's reach. The resulting information proximity meant once again "my" information belonged to "me."

But it didn't stop there. The ever greater presence of silicon and personal interconnection means that increasingly the data belongs to "us." This world of information intimacy is interdependent and ephemeral. It builds on relationships between people rather than companies and institutions. It also places the spotlight firmly on trust between the individuals and institutions that now share each other's information.

The technology we use to sustain those relationships is also changing. We are walking an evolutionary path from a world of largely verbal communications, based on text and data, to a world of visual and virtual communications where the richness of interaction is increased exponentially (Fig. 1.1). A picture is worth a thousand words. Be prepared for ever-increasing levels of personal intimacy over the World Wide Web!

The availability of data about "us" and the increasing richness of the communications channels mean that we can become smarter in expressing our

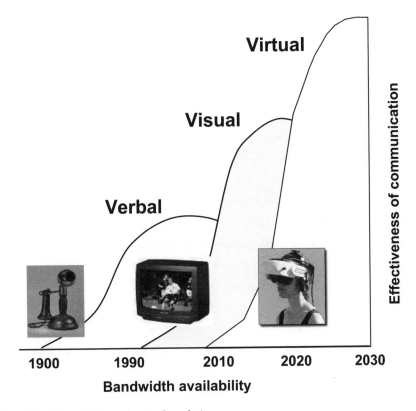

Fig. 1.1 The verbal–visual–virtual revolution.

needs and aspirations as individuals. *Consumers are becoming increasingly pre-occupied with the quest for their own personal experiences rather than a company's discrete products or services.* The new mantra is to "be," to "go," to "know," to "do" and to "have fun." And these experience-based desires cannot be met simply by single-point solutions, be they products or services. Something has to change.

The unchanging corporation

While the customer is looking at the horizon, today's corporation is too often still focused firmly inward, just as it has been for the past two centuries. We still see vast marketing departments trying to mold consumers' demands to the product, rather than molding the product to meet the consumer's demands. We see companies operating within linear supply chains with static ongoing customer–supplier relationships. And we see multiple layers of management trained to deal with the complexities of co-ordinating these monolithic structures.

But the proliferation and richness of interactive channels mean that individuals of all types, consumers and employees, are able to express for the first time their individual lifestyle needs and preferences. It is only a matter of time before the stubborn old product-centric corporations begin to suffer at the hands of these empowered individuals.

And it's not just consumer demand that has been reshaped by the introduction of the silicon chip. Traditional supplier–customer relationships are being broken down by the rapid proliferation of electronic markets who seek to disintermediate established players. Instead of inflexible, linear supply chains extending from raw materials to finished goods, we see a transition to more dispersed webs of business relationships designed to respond quickly and effectively to emerging individual needs.

But maybe the biggest worry for today's management is the investor who increasingly wants to see companies responding to the many radical challenges of the connected economy. Having emerged from one of the longest bull markets in history, investors around the globe are showing increasing impatience with both new and old economy stocks, and are demanding a bold response to the opportunities of the future. They know that competitive advantage can no longer be sustained by producing more and better "stuff," and we have seen the value of some of the world's most successful corporations, old and new, halved in a matter of months.

The realization that the present waves of technological innovation will continue with ever-greater frequency has persuaded investors to include a "future growth options" component in their calculations (Fig. 1.2). They want companies to show just how they are prepared to cope with the inevitability of change. And, so far, few old economy corporations have been able to demonstrate convincingly such new growth options.

Valuing "future opportunities" is part of the answer, but it's still not enough. There is a growing awareness of the mess that some attempts to do this produced during the dot.com boom. IT and Internet companies rode high on future growth expectations for several years, but many failed to deliver tangible outcomes and, eventually, their stock was savaged as a result. Those who invested money in the dot.com boom will know only too well the consequences of ignoring positive cash flows.

Relational capital and the connected economy

We think the most important and sustainable source of shareholder value in a connected economy will be something more fundamental. It will be the net-

Shareholder value =	NPV of existing business model	+	Future growth options
Uncertainty	• Low		• High
Performance indicators	• Lagging • Financial		• Leading • Non-financial
Key drivers & intangibles	• Efficiency • Current products & related brands		• Innovation • Flexibility • Ability to execute
Tools & techniques	• DCF/ EVA/ROI		• Real option frameworks e.g. decision trees, simulation etc.

With kind permission from Ernst & Young

Fig. 1.2   Share value includes tangible and intangible elements.

work of relationships that a company has created and will go on to create over time. Every large company today has many thousands or even millions of valued relationships with its customers, suppliers, shareholders and employees. We call this *relational capital* – the monetary value of these current and future relationships.

We will explain later exactly how to use the powerful new information infrastructures to unlock relational capital and demonstrate how you can estimate its value. We even propose a simple formula that shows how future shareholder wealth can be linked to a company's relationship-building capabilities. The four main factors involved here are customer intimacy, alliance building, corporate agility and trust.

The upshot of this is that instead of being product or service centric, tomorrow's corporations will be relationship centric. And the implications of this change cannot be overstated. You may not read about the position of Chief Relationship Officer in today's corporate prospectuses but it may turn out to be one of the critical posts in the successful firms of the future. The key to the creation of value will be the ability to form and re-form alliances and to sustain high levels of trust.

The corporate envelope

Firms have been growing in scale for as long as we can remember. But the trend towards mergers, which accelerated throughout the 1990s, has reached its final frontier. We argue that getting larger is not the answer. Most mergers are a waste of shareholder time and money and we think that this is going to be even truer in the years ahead. Getting bigger only succeeds in increasing internal costs and reducing agility – precisely the opposite of what companies will need to do if they are to survive in the future.

Firms have been trying to get sleeker and slimmer. They've re-engineered themselves, they've installed ERP systems, and they've paid fortunes to get a step ahead of the pack. But all they have managed to achieve was a slight reduction in internal transaction costs and maximized efficiency of output. They missed the big prize because they looked at processes and information inside the firm's boundaries, instead of solving the problems across the entire supply chain.

The revolution brought about by e-commerce will bring some further improvements in internal costs, but the most dramatic effects will eventually manifest themselves in a rapid fall in external transaction costs. Electronic marketplaces will be the primary agents of greatly enhanced connectivity outside the corporation and they will eventually facilitate a massive change in the character of the supply chain.

Why does this matter? It has been known for seventy years that the size of the firm is largely governed by a balance – where the costs of doing business externally are equal to the costs of doing something in-house. Rapid falls in external transaction costs will make it possible to reduce the size of the firm to increase agility and unlock shareholder value.

A combination of causes

These are some of the forces of change pulling on today's corporations. It's time for firms to get themselves ready to respond, but most of them are still too centered on their products and their internal functions. They need to recognize how consumer demand is being changed by the empowering effect of greater choice and price transparency, at the same time the demand is becoming more interpretable because of more interactive distribution channels. And they should prepare themselves for the serious disruption to traditional supply chains as powerful new information infrastructures propel businesses towards more flexible webs of trading relationships.

First and foremost, they need a new focus on agility, and as you can't be big and agile at the same time (the internal cost of movement is too high), fragmentation is looking more and more attractive. And breaking up has never been easier. The availability and breadth of communications channels between organizations is growing exponentially, which is sharply reducing the costs of doing business.

And let's not overlook the force of the push from inside – from the CEO who needs to do something, no matter how radical, to deliver results to institutional shareholders.

Taken together, these forces are a fundamental challenge to the structures of the mega-corporations that inhabit the Global 2000. It's not the first time the business world has undergone major upheaval – the only corporation in the US top hundred list of 1900 to see in the new millennium was General Electric. But we think this revolutionary cycle, as well as being ongoing, will be far shorter and more brutal than its predecessors.

For those who embrace the coming change, the prize in terms of unlocked relational capital will be enormous. But be prepared for a breathless turnaround. It may be another ten years before the economy has mutated recognizably into its new state but it's going to feel like snowboarding in front of an avalanche.

THE ATOMIC AGE

Introducing the atoms

Business success in the future will come from excelling in just one of four dimensions (Fig. 1.3). Our atomic theory evolves directly from this fundamental assertion and identifies six types of individual atomic entities within these four dimensions:

- **Innovation:** the engines of the economy will be small, knowledge-intensive *smart companies* that create a constant stream of innovative new offerings – combining bundles of products and services, and deriving value from their know-how and peer-to-peer interactions
- **Relationships:** we foresee two types of atom emerging here – *customer managers* will understand the desires of consumers, while *webspinners* will mediate the relationship between the supplier and the customer at each stage in the supply chain and emerging value webs. Together they will assemble the goods and services required to meet each customer's individual demand.
- **Assets:** someone still has to manufacture detergents and refine the oil. *Asset platforms* will deliver global economies of scope and scale in areas such as manufacturing and logistics, while *service platforms* will manage

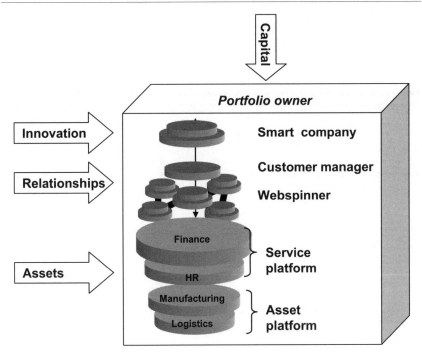

Fig. 1.3   The atomizing corporation.

    process-related activities like human relations, procurement and finance
across a variety of sectors

- **Capital:** shareholders will reap the rewards from the unlocking of relational capital as giant corporations are transformed into *portfolio owners*,
holding equity in the atomic companies they have spawned.

Atoms and supporting electronic marketplaces may be individually small and
incomplete, but the full power of our theory is that they can combine into systems, or molecules, that are powerful, fast and immensely flexible, and still
manage to completely meet customer expectations.

    The ebbing tide of vertical, or sector-specific, marketplaces will leave
behind rich communications channels that drive down the costs of doing business by streamlining and, in many cases, transforming the supply chain. These
lower external transaction costs will themselves play a part in the atomization
of giant corporations, while the process of atomization will in turn boost the
importance of these marketplaces as enablers of trade.

In Table 1.1, we lay out some of the parameters that we would expect to see in our atoms by the end of the decade (see Chapter 10 for details).

Table 1.1 Atomic types and stock market values.

Atom type	Manpower	Profitability (dividend yield)	Likely P/E ratio	Scope	Primary assets
Asset platform	Low thousands	2.2–5.6%	11–18	Global, within an industry	Physical property
Service platform	Hundreds– low thousands	1.5–3.3%	23–33	Within a legal system	Process expertise
Webspinner	100–200	1.5–2.5%	60–150	Global	Business relationships
Customer manager	100–200	1.5–3.5%	40–80	Within a customer group	Consumer intimacy
Smart company	1–100	0.0–0.4%	0–200	Highly specialized	Intellectual property
Portfolio owner	10–100	1.2–1.8%	70–110	Global	Other atoms

Where do the atoms come from?

While some of the atoms will be new entities, particularly the relationship-based "customer managers" and "webspinners," most will be spun off from today's large corporations.

Think of a corporation as an apple sliced into layers (Fig. 1.4):

- The *governance layer* of the corporation corresponds to the board and perhaps their immediate reports. It makes decisions about strategy, oversight and alliance management, and we see this as becoming a *portfolio owner* atom, acting as the means by which released relational capital is returned to investors.
- *Specific business elements* are the core processes that differentiate our corporation from its peers, in terms of intellectual property, design and pro-

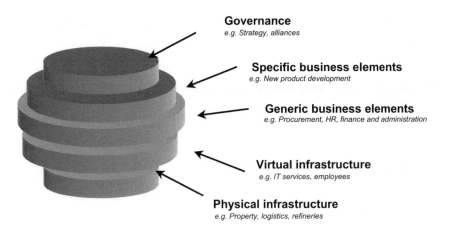

Governance
e.g. Strategy, alliances

Specific business elements
e.g. New product development

Generic business elements
e.g. Procurement, HR, finance and administration

Virtual infrastructure
e.g. IT services, employees

Physical infrastructure
e.g. Property, logistics, refineries

Fig. 1.4 Layers of the corporation.

cess knowledge. This layer of the corporation will become *smart companies*, *customer managers* and *webspinners*.

■ The *generic business elements* which make up the majority of the corporation's processes and which are "just part of how we do business," will be externalized either through outsourcing or joint ventures. Processes such as procurement, HR, finance, accounting, IT etc, will become *service platforms*.

■ The *virtual infrastructure* elements are used to support the generic processes of the business, like office space, computer and communications hardware and software. These will migrate into *service platform* or *asset platform* atoms, depending on their strategic importance to the corporation.

■ Most corporations, with the exception of those purely in the service industries, have considerable amounts of capital invested in *physical infrastructure* – assembly lines, refineries, trucks, warehouses – and these will be the basis of *asset platform* atoms.

Some atoms will spring forth from corporations fully formed, while others will be created from the best elements of consortia. Either way, we think that if an asset or a process represents *what* the corporation does then it should be retained, but if it represents something that is part of *how* it does it, then it should be sold or disbanded.

This is a radical vision – to accept it means you will have to ask yourself what it is that you and only you do best, and then letting go of everything else. But that "everything else" is a source of potential value – it will be possible to unbundle these things from the corporation both as a source of (relational) capital worth and as a potential cost saving.

ATOMS, MOLECULES AND BONDS

In this book, we talk about "atomic corporations" and "molecular economies," but what are atoms and molecules, and what is the relevance to our business world?

Atoms are the basic building blocks of the elements, making up everything we see around us. There are more than 100 types of element in rows and columns of the periodic table.

You rarely find atoms on their own because they are much more familiar in partnerships called molecules. Molecules can range from two atoms, like the oxygen that we breathe, to millions of atoms in the DNA that carries our genetic code.

But it takes more than atoms to make a molecule. You also need bonds that crystallize, in effect, the relationship between the atoms. Building these bonds takes energy and the larger the molecule the more energy is invested in this relationship building. The process that we call life is about creation of more complex molecules by burning the various sources of energy. (Perhaps the process that we call mergers is about creating larger companies by burning shareholder value!)

Back to the chemistry: all the energy invested in the relationship can be released when the bonds are broken. With a little help from a spark, the internal combustion engine turns large hydrocarbon molecules into much smaller units like carbon dioxide and water, and the released energy makes our vehicles move.

And that's the theme of the book. We think that, with the right spark, we can break up the mega-corporations of today into simpler units, releasing the energy into the economy in the form of relational capital.

Atoms and individuals

And what about you, the individual? In a world where intangible assets and relational capital are much more important, individual wealth will depend on knowledge, relationships and personal brand. Mental agility and trust will be regarded as the most important qualities driving personal wealth. We will, in effect, become our own *smart company* or innovative thinker, and *webspinner* or relationship builder.

The infrastructural elements of our lives such as mobility, accommodation, healthcare and financial management will be supported by personal *service platform* providers, accessed via individual *customer managers*. We already have twenty-four hour concierge services aimed at the highly paid, doing their shopping, laundering their shirts, and taking as much of the effort out of daily existence as possible. In our future, a much wider group of affluent employees will employ many such service providers to simplify their day-to-day affairs.

And what about the employment contracts of tomorrow? Life-long employment with one or two corporations is over, even if some quarters of Europe and Asia have not realized it yet. Don't expect anyone to be looking after your interests in this New World. Atomic corporations will only value their employees for as long as they meet their requirements of any one moment in time. Welcome to transaction employment.

Scary as this might sound it is a good thing if you have any entrepreneurial spirit. The atomic corporation will generously reward you if it can understand how and where you fit into the new business world. Our real incomes are already at least double those of our parents and the prospect of a million-dollar salary is not unrealistic for anyone reading this book.

THE STRUCTURE OF THE BOOK

Part II – Discontinuities

In the next section of the book we will explain why atomization is not only desirable but inevitable. We look at the evolution of the large corporation and the forces that shape it, changes in the nature of its relationship with individuals, and the effects of the continuing growth of technology. If you a regular reader of this kind of book, you may already know a lot of the stuff in this section. If so, you can skip straight to the *Drivers* or *Destination* sections.

■ Chapter 2, *Land of the Giants*, looks at the mega-corporations that roam the economic landscape today. We will look at the factors that drove company formation in the industrial age, why they have grown to their current size, and why we think they have been going in the wrong direction.

■ Chapter 3, *Towards a New-World Context*, discusses the four main forces of change that are fashioning the new economy – technology, the social agenda, economics and politics, and considers their effect on both the individual and the corporation of the twenty-first century.

■ Chapter 4, *A Revolution in Digital Connectivity*, looks at the development of communications technologies as we move from a verbal world into an increasingly visual and, later, virtual world. By exploiting the richness and reach of the evolving World Wide Web, each one of us will be able to access, absorb and transmit an unrivalled amount of information on every aspect of our professional and domestic lives.

Part III – Drivers

While the previous section described the external factors that make atomization both possible and desirable, *Drivers* describes the internal factors that will make corporations want to change. Shareholder expectations are mounting, and management is under pressure to unlock value from new sources of corporate wealth. The assets are already sweating; most new sources of value are likely to emerge from current relationships and knowledge assets.

■ Chapter 5, *New Sources of Shareholder Wealth*, describes the valuation of traditional and new economy companies, and argues that both are flawed. We present a formula for combining physical and intangible value that looks forward to our whirlwind future.

■ Chapter 6, *Relational Capital*, is the first of the elements that are unique to this book. Given that relationships generate increasing value in a connected economy, the most sustainable source of shareholder value is the network of relationships that a company has created and will subsequently create over time. We introduce the idea of relational capital and look at the value of trust in the New World.

Part IV – Destination

Having laid out the forces for atomization, *Destination* now presents our views on how the new economy will be constructed.

■ Chapter 7, *Let's Meet the Atoms*, describes our atom types in more detail, with examples of what services they will provide and where we might see them supporting each other.

■ Chapter 8, *Making the Molecules Work*, looks at the communications channels that will link the new players to each other and to their customers, and shows how we think the atomised version of the global economy will work, including regulatory and tax issues.

■ Chapter 9, *Atomizing the Corporation*, will tell you how to find sources of relational capital hidden in your organization, and how atoms can be identified. It presents two methods of finding atoms, the first by layer and the second by a detailed examination of its components

■ Chapter 10, *Atomic Numbers*, is a companion to Chapter 9 and looks at success factors for these atoms, how they should be managed, and what their value will be. It talks about how to draw up outline balance sheets and profit and loss accounts for each of the atoms. It will answer questions like:

  ■ How big will the atoms be?
  ■ What skills do the people in the atoms need?
  ■ Who will manage them?
  ■ What happens to the corporate brand? and
  ■ What will the atoms be worth?

■ Chapter 11, *Industrial (R)evolution* posits that the only value of a theory is its ability to predict results, and looks at an atomic version of some of our major industries. It covers financial services (both retail and corporate), the energy sector, telecommunications, consumer products and information technology.

■ Chapter 12, *New Partnerships, New Wealth*, looks at how corporations develop ideas to protect the core, extend their reach, and do something totally new. It presents alliances and consortia as a means of unlocking the relational capital.

Part V – Destiny

■ Chapter 13, *The Atomized Individual*, examines individual values in a connected society. As corporations atomize into their core competencies, so you will be encouraged to do likewise. You will seek the appropriate atomic structures where your competencies are best exploited. You will also look to subcontract out those activities of little personal value or competency – such as domestic arrangements.

AN INVITATION TO THE FUTURE

Our canvas is perhaps larger than that of most business books. The changes that we are talking about are huge. They will also affect every one of us in the developed world in both our roles as consumers and producers of wealth. As consumers, we will have far more choice, and at far lower cost, than ever before. As employees (or employers) we will find that flexibility will bring freedom and rewards.

Those of you who are working for large corporations today have a world of opportunity facing you, if you surf the tidal wave of change rather than trying to stop it. To those in colleges about to enter the job market, we urge you to think of your career not as a ladder but as a road with more than one destination.

We are all about to find out what that old Chinese proverb about "living in interesting times" really means. We hope the insights offered here will help you to navigate your professional life towards a more productive and harmonious future.

Our thoughts on the Atomic Corporation are still developing, and we would welcome your insights. Talk to us, and to each other, at http://www.atomiccorp.com/, where you can find news, updates to the figures, and case studies of atomizing corporations.

PART II
Discontinuities

The historical forces that have driven corporations into their current shape have not just slowed down, they have gone into sharp reverse. When information flowed from the corporation to the consumer, size meant muscle. Two-way connectivity gives power back to the individual, and corporate ears are now more important than corporate brawn.

How have we reached this watershed? Let's explore why corporations have got to be the shape they are, and why and how the technical, social and economic situation has changed. It's time for the corporation to change too.

CHAPTER 2

Land of the Giants

INTRODUCTION

I N THIS SECTION OF THE BOOK, *Discontinuities*, we lay the groundwork that will explain why atomization is not only desirable but inevitable. We will look at the evolution of the large corporation and the forces that shape it, changes in the nature of its relationship with individuals and the effects of the continuing growth of technology.

But before we start on the history we need to have a look at our geography. After all, we can't predict the destination without knowing the starting point. We are on the verge of the most fundamental change that the world's economy has seen in 40 years. Just one decade from now, the young observer will look back at the economic landscape of the mid-nineties in bewilderment, not understanding why or how it worked. We need to understand why he will be bewildered, and to do that we need to be comfortable with the lie of the land. So we will look at the giants that roam the landscape today – the mega-corporations. We will look at the factors that drove company value in the industrial age, and what made successful corporations successful. We will discuss why businesses form, why they have grown to their current size, and why we think they have been going in the wrong direction.

And then we will tell you why they will break apart.

WHY DO CORPORATIONS FORM?

The cost of doing business

Received wisdom has it that entrepreneurs start businesses when they believe they see an efficient way of converting inputs (raw materials, knowledge, labor) into more valuable outputs (products, services etc.).

The shape and boundaries of a business are governed by a single question, asked about each of the things that it uses to create its outputs or which it consumes in order to keep itself operating: *should it manufacture the thing itself or buy it in?*

Make-or-buy decisions are governed by two factors:

- *price* – "what is the price of this component?" and
- *transaction cost* – "what does it cost me to buy this component in addition to the price?"

The price factor is easy to understand, but we will use an example to illustrate the transaction cost element.

Let's imagine that you are an entrepreneur that wants to buy something, perhaps a set of tires to put on a bicycle that you are manufacturing in your garage. You'll need to identify potential suppliers for the tires and find out who offers the best prices – a process that consumes your time and manpower as well as that of the potential suppliers.

Once you have decided who should be on your shortlist, you can negotiate a contract, order the tires, and pay your supplier's invoice. Finally, you will need a way of managing the supplier so that any problems in the relationship can be sorted out and so that you have the flexibility to switch suppliers if conditions change. Thus we can see that the total cost to you is the price of the tires themselves added to other, smaller, drains on your pocket and your time. We will group them into:

- *discovery costs*: deciding what you are going to buy and who you are going to buy from;
- *sourcing costs*: the costs associated with drawing up a contract, buying goods against it, delivery, payment etc., and any switching costs associated with the change to this new supplier; and
- *contract policing costs*: managing the supplier relationship, resorting to law if it all goes wrong, renegotiating etc.

Of course the supplier has equivalent costs and it will come as no surprise that it is usually the buyer that picks up the tab for these functions as well. Don't be fooled into thinking that any of these costs are negligible. Think about how many people in your place of work are involved in transaction support (the procurement department, the accounts department, the lawyers and just about everybody who buys or sells anything). For really high-priced items like an airplane or a battleship these costs can easily run into tens of millions of dollars.

Vertical integration and the need for capital

You will usually decide to buy your tires from the supplier whose price was right – provided they were not too hard to deal with. But what if you can't find a price you're prepared to pay, or the pain of making the purchase was too great? If you think that you can make the tires more cheaply yourself, you might choose to raise some capital and build a tire plant in the garden shed.

Now that sounds like an insane thing to do but there is a notable precedent in the annals. Ford Motor did just that – it owned its own rubber plantation just to make sure its assembly lines never ran out of tires, in addition to its own iron ore mines.

It can make sense to extend your reach up or down the supply chain if the cost of guaranteeing supply is high, or if you can raise capital more cheaply than your suppliers. And conversely, there are circumstances when you might want to let someone else handle parts of your core business if they can deliver it more cheaply than you.

We mentioned cost of capital just now, but it is no longer that important. In the earliest days of industrialization, the greatest barrier to corporation formation was the lack of money to invest in new ideas and new plant.[1] But as the overall wealth of the economy grows and there is more money around to invest, the "capital barrier" becomes less and less relevant. Apart from the really capital-intensive businesses, which we'll come to in Chapter 7, it isn't a factor any more.

FORD MOTOR COMPANY

Henry Ford started production of the Model T at his factory in Highland Park in 1913. It was made out of standardized components assembled on a moving production line, an innovation in the infant car industry at the time.

Originally, Ford bought the components from external suppliers, but soon started to produce them in-house. Not only did Ford think he could make the components cheaper and more efficiently than his suppliers, but perhaps more importantly he wanted increased control over their supply. Massive demand for his cars meant he needed parts produced in greater volumes, and improvements in design meant he needed them made to more precise levels of quality than ever before.

In 1927 the River Rouge complex was opened in Dearborn. It had a steel mill, a glass factory and produced everything needed to build the new Model A car. Soon, control was to extend beyond the manufacture of individual components all the way to the raw materials themselves. Ford bought iron ore mines in Minnesota and rubber plantations in Brazil, as well as ships and railroads to deliver the materials unimpeded straight to the factory.

As the telephone started to reduce external transaction costs in the late 1940s and early 1950s, Ford sold off many of its raw material assets, but continued to manufacture its own components until the 1990s.

In the light of increased competition and success of Japanese manufacturers, Ford revisited its operational strategy. All component suppliers have been restructured into a single enterprise, Visteon, with the intention of spinning it off as a separate business.

Attention is now moving further up the value chain, towards sales, maintenance and repair of its vehicles where the margins are much greater. Approaching its centenary in 2003, Ford wants to be seen as a provider of automotive products and services rather than just a maker of cars.

Internal costs and the Coase Equilibrium

Of course, there are transaction costs associated with the "make" decisions, as well. If you do want to run your own tire plant you will need to "discover" good people to hire, "source" them and "police" their behavior.

As the organization gets larger and expands beyond your span of control, you will need to hire layers of management to oversee it. This further increases your costs, as you have to find a way – which we generally call "management reporting" – of overcoming the political infighting and isolation from reality that these layers of management cause.[2] The larger the firm gets, the higher these internal costs get and the less agile the firms become. Everyone reading this who has worked for a large firm knows the frustration of getting things done internally, and has at some time probably gone to outside suppliers because it's faster or cheaper than getting the job done in-house.

The key point here is this: the balance of what you do, and what you let others do for you, depends on the relative "pain" of trading or doing things yourself. Each of these "pains" is composed of two elements – price and trans-action cost. So here is our first general rule – *firms expand until the internal costs are equal to the cost of transacting externally*. This equilibrium is illus-trated in Figure 2.1.

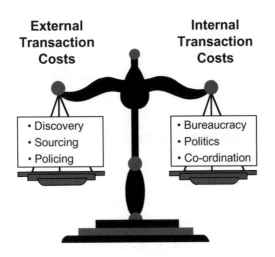

Fig. 2.1   The Coase Equilibrium.

This insight may be vitally important, but it isn't particularly new. It was first published in 1937 by Nobel laureate, Ronald Coase.[3] Since then, a whole school of Transaction Cost Economics has been founded around it[4] and other writers have extended Coase's work to look at how other institutions,[5] such as bank clearing houses, commodity markets etc., arise in order to economize on transaction cost.

Are supply chains stable?

In the earlier example, you were buying a single set of tires for a single bicycle. If making bicycles is your business, it's pretty clear that contracting separately for each set of tires is not an efficient way to operate, and you will probably try to do a deal with a supplier covering a certain number of tires at a pre-agreed price. This eliminates uncertainty in the price and removes some of the transaction costs, and you now have a supply chain!

So we can say that supply chains reduce transaction costs and minimize potential price variation.

If the difference in prices between suppliers is likely to be less than the cost of switching to a new one, you might never change suppliers at all. The converse also applies: if the price of rubber was very volatile, suppliers would have bought their stocks at different times and there could well be considerable variations in the market price of tires. If this is the case, then individual renegotiation for each set of tires becomes more sensible. Of course, we have developed Futures and Options markets as a way of fixing the price and capping the transaction costs, but it seems to be true that *price volatility undermines stable supply chains*.

MERGERS – MORE OFTEN WRONG THAN RIGHT?

Why merge?

So one alternative to contracting for every set of tires is to guarantee supply by buying one of your suppliers. That's what Ford did and it's what mergers are often designed to achieve. It is part of what was happening throughout the 1990s, when many of our giant and not-so-giant corporations struggled to buy each other in a seemingly never-ending series of mergers and acquisitions (M&As). The annual value of merger transactions around the world increased in value from about $400bn in 1991 to approximately $3500bn in 2000.

But there is a whole range of other reasons for M&A activity. We shall ignore the voices of the cynics who say that the primary reason for a merger is to swell CEO egos or enrich the investment banker that suggested it in the first place, and use the words of Smith and Sadtler,[6] who tell us that the usual reasons for M&As are:

- potential for operating synergies (e.g. elimination of duplicated cost through staff reductions);
- to increase control over the target market by absorbing potential competition;
- reach critical mass;[7]
- acquire a critical skill or technology (as long as the "skills" don't walk out of the door);
- gain access to new markets or to a global production base;
- de-risk the business by balancing the asset portfolio (e.g. buying corporations in different stages of maturity, geographies and industries);
- guarantee means of supply or distribution by vertical integration; and
- fend off an acquisition threat by buying a large company (the "Poison Pill" defense).

These explanations have been all well and good in the past (in a world where external transaction costs will forever remain high) but they don't always look so convincing in the context of our radically changing business environment. Controlling markets, acquiring critical skills or technologies, accessing new markets or a global production base, and guaranteeing the means of supply or distribution can also be achieved through alliances. Mergers increase corporate size, which as we know usually increases internal costs disproportionately. Alliances would seem to be preferable if the transaction costs are not excessive.

There is no shortage of research to support this skepticism about the value of much M&A activity. In a study of 33 corporations and more than 3700 merger transactions by Michael Porter,[8] the vast majority of acquired corporations had been sold off after a few years, leading to the conclusion that the acquisitions had been failures. Porter said the effect was clearest where businesses had strayed into areas they did not understand.

Going the wrong way

Therefore we would expect mergers to work only when there are significant economies of scale in capital investment – a theme which we will build on when we discuss business platforms in Chapter 7 – or where significant reductions of internal costs can be achieved.

And indeed most M&As do fail. Far less than one-fifth of mergers create substantial returns for shareholders and a half actually destroy shareholder value (Fig. 2.2).

Some failures are, of course, just the result of bad decisions. Unnecessary diversification, a bad purchase perhaps resulting from poor due diligence, or lack of experience of M&As are often to blame. And other, seemingly sensible, mergers fall apart because of simple integration failures.

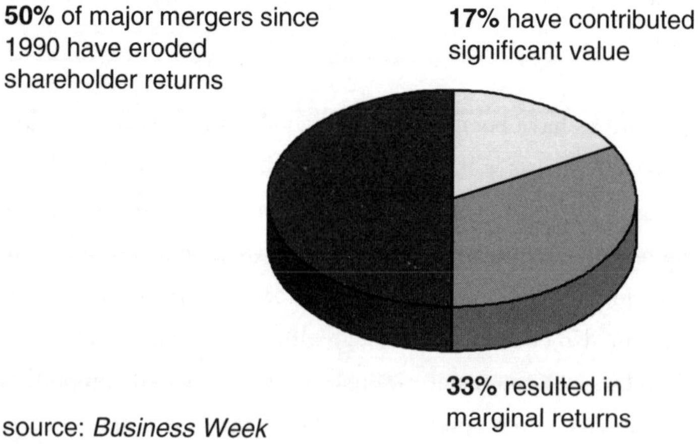

50% of major mergers since 1990 have eroded shareholder returns

17% have contributed significant value

33% resulted in marginal returns

source: *Business Week*

Fig. 2.2   Most mergers erode shareholder value.

Very few corporations make a success of the M&A process. To pull it off you not only have to make the right decision about who to buy but you must also flawlessly execute the post-merger integration program.

Most acquirers implement post-merger integration programs that do not go far enough, or fast enough, in taking out internal costs. Indeed, new internal costs (in the form of political infighting) are all too often a result of a merger of equals, as anyone who has been through such an exercise will tell you.

One proven winner at the M&A game is Cisco Systems (discussed further in Chapter 6), which has a well-established process for acquisitions. Cisco avoids the trap of increasing internal costs by ruthlessly imposing its own processes and systems on the acquired company. (At the other end of the spectrum is the merged insurer who changed the name of the corporation but took integration no further than re-engineering the letterhead.)

Ultimately, one has to question whether the rush to increase size is a good thing at all. In the words of Cisco Systems, "The old model of owning and controlling all links in the supply chain now creates friction, forestalls nimbleness within the corporation and consumes resources better applied elsewhere."[9]

Not all mergers fail, and some are necessary for reasons of scale, but on the whole they increase internal costs and distract corporations from external dangers. That may have been fine in the 1990s, but times have changed.

RE-ENGINEERED TO DEATH

Re-engineering as a fashion statement

Now let's turn to the other great corporate fad, re-engineering. Over the past three decades, corporations have become much more – perhaps too much more – efficient, perhaps to the point where they lack sufficient spare resources to respond to changes in external conditions. Management consultants should take most of the responsibility for this (good and bad).

In the seventies, consultants introduced the idea of the "perfect business function" and promoted certain corporate absolutes like standardized finance and accounting operations across the globe. This introduction of best practice helped eliminate bureaucracy and waste, and was (on the whole) a good thing to do.

The eighties brought an increased focus on efficiency. We recognized, for example, that the actions needed to process an invoice spanned the boundaries of these new functions, and consultants responded with process re-engineering. This changed the way that internal processes were viewed and further reduced waste, albeit often fairly brutally. The end result was much leaner operations but the ultimate benefits were marginal. Everyone was doing the same thing. Re-engineering exercises left no sustained competitive advantage, as every other corporation was forced into them to compete.

In the nineties, we saw the recognition that cross-boundary processes were failing because the staff did not have sufficient visibility of information to make decisions. The result was the almost ubiquitous, and not always successful, introduction of ERP systems.

The re-engineering trend continues, but under different names. In the last five years we have been tearing down national boundaries inside multinational corporations to pursue economies of scale, and more recently, we have started to see the introduction of Web-enabled processes to further enhance internal efficiency and speed.

THE GROWING CONSULTING SECTOR

From modest beginnings early last century to a multi-billion-dollar industry, consulting has become one of the most dynamic growth sectors in the new economy. Fuelled by technology-driven change, there is every prospect that the sector will continue to prosper and evolve for several decades to come.

In its early form, consulting emerged in the 1930s as a service to manufacturing industry. The main offering was work-study measurement, designed to identify and overcome inadequate work practices on the shop floor. A science based on improving factory performance emerged as a consequence, and several consulting firms such as Urwicks and PE-International grew to prominence. These techniques predated computer automation by two or more decades.

By the sixties a new group of influential firms emerged to focus on broader corporate policy and planning issues fuelled by structural changes taking place in the world economy. These included now familiar names such as McKinsey, A.T. Kearney and Booz Allen Hamilton. Access to the boardroom became a by-product of these strategy boutiques. At the same time a further group of management advisors focused on technology-driven issues. These included names such as Arthur D Little, PA Consulting and SRI International.

With the explosive growth of information technology throughout the manufacturing and service industries in the seventies, the major five accounting firms diversified into management consulting. Despite consolidations and spin-offs, these firms continue to occupy leadership positions in this segment of the consulting services market. In addition to IT, privatizations of national utilities and telecommunications companies gave these firms a welcome boost.

In 1990, Business Re-engineering – a by-product of MIT's "Management in the Nineties" program, spawned yet a further wave of consulting boutiques such as Index and Gemini as well as a mainstream response by the larger houses. This wave has been followed by e-business almost a decade later, and a subsequent group of start-ups such as Sapient, Scient and Viant (referred to as the fast five for their meteoric rise and rapid descent).

As the consulting business matures, the inevitable rounds of mergers and acquisitions have taken place leaving a handful of full-service providers such as Accenture, CAP Gemini Ernst & Young and PriceWaterhouseCoopers. Other global contenders include the remaining independent strategy houses and many niche players.

There is a world beyond the corporate horizon

All this corporate rewiring, streamlining, and redesign had the effect of reducing the costs of internal operations. And, in turn, this reduced internal transaction costs, which reinforced the structural status quo and should, in theory, help firms to survive and even grow larger.

But corporations don't exist in a vacuum. Take the accounts payable function we talked about earlier, for example. It spans not just internal boundaries but also some of the corporation's suppliers and maybe a bank or two. An efficient process would, of course, extend information visibility to these entities as well.

In the real world, even the links between the Accounts Receivable system of the supplier and the Accounts Payable system of the customer are almost always implemented using paper. Corporations implementing these state-of-the-art ERP systems increasingly became islands of automation in a sea of poor practice.

Kicking management consultants for this omission, although tempting, is hardly fair – there was little choice but to take an internal focus. Apart from painful implementations of electronic data interchange (EDI[10]), there was no mechanism to share information and delegation across corporate boundaries.

In summary, re-engineering was a fine idea but it didn't and perhaps couldn't go far enough. Deeper efficiency could only have been achieved by extending the redesign beyond the corporation's immediate control. But now there is the opportunity to do just that. The new, richer interconnectivity between corporations means we can at last concentrate on the re-engineering of the entire supply chain.

UPSETTING THE APPLE CART – B2B E-COMMERCE

Cost reductions

We started this chapter with a discussion of transaction costs, internal and external, and how they govern corporation size. Since then, we have looked at mergers and re-engineering, which respectively increase and decrease internal transaction costs. To complete the picture, let's take a look at the ways new technology can slash transaction costs and prices.

This is not a new idea either. Coase pointed out in 1937 that "changes like the telephone and telegraph" were likely to make it possible for geographically dispersed corporations to co-ordinate their activities[11] and we can see how better telephony, IT systems and air travel have made possible the global corporations of today.

Up until the 1990s, communication outside the firm was difficult. Even now, with the Internet seemingly everywhere, "customer contact" mostly consists of throwing information at the customer in an artificial attempt to create a market for the product. Similarly, communications up and down the supply chain are all too often implemented using slow, low-bandwidth paper.

It's easy to see why corporations focus on internal factors like efficiency of production when the external feedback is so poor. But times have changed. Processes within corporations are getting sleeker as intranets start to spread knowledge and functionality across the organization, and business-to-business (B2B) interaction has been unrecognizably transformed by the Internet.

Let's look again at the composition of external transaction costs and how the Web affects them.

- *Discovery costs*: deciding who you are going to buy from is made much easier when electronic catalogues and auctions give almost-complete visibility of suppliers and their prices.
- *Sourcing costs*: vertical and horizontal marketplaces should standardize, and thus sharply reduce, the costs associated with contracting and doing business. This standardization also reduces switching costs.
- *Contract policing costs*: when it is easy to see how previous customers have rated a supplier (and vice versa), peer pressure becomes an efficient way of enforcing contracts.

So we can see that B2B e-commerce, as manifested by standards such as XML and new channels such as vertical marketplaces,[12] has the potential to sharply reduce the cost of doing business with another corporation.

Internal costs are falling at the same time for similar reasons. Enabling internal processes on the Internet eliminates some of the bureaucracy and improves information flows (although they may not do much about internal politics!). But the real benefits will stem from the steeper drop in external costs. The effect of Web-enabled transformation has been slower to reach these out-facing relationships, which means the external costs have further to fall.

And the implication of this asymmetric decline is pretty stark – if external transaction costs fall faster than internal costs, the market inefficiencies which prop up corporate structures will be eliminated and the boundaries of the firm are again open to question.

Price reductions

All this information visibility amounts to an epitaph for the traditional model of the supply chain, where the supplier sets the price and the consumer duly pays up. To start with, the relationship between all the parties has been radically altered by new levels of connectivity and the resulting efficiency benefits. Secondly, the Internet has seriously boosted purchasing power through the aggregation of demand, price transparency, and virtual auctioning. And the consequences are far-reaching. Cheaper transaction costs will shake the established corporate boundaries, while supply chains themselves are destabilized by new degrees of price volatility. This conjunction is one of the main dynamics behind the pressure to atomize existing corporate structures.

RECAP

We've covered a lot of ground in this chapter, and it might be worth recapping the main points.

- The size of the firm is largely governed by the point at which the internal costs of doing something (politics, bureaucracy, information obfuscation) balance the costs of doing it outside the firm (discovery, sourcing, policing).
- Re-engineering and ERP systems have focused on reducing internal transaction costs and maximizing efficiency of output. But they generally looked at processes and information inside the firm's boundaries, reinforcing the corporate envelope.
- Getting larger is not the answer – nearly three-quarters of mergers don't deliver significant value. Many, perhaps most, M&As succeed in increasing internal costs and reducing competitiveness.

■ E-commerce will bring some reductions in internal costs but a much sharper reduction in external transaction costs. This sweeps away the market inefficiencies that prop up corporate structures and thus destabilizes the boundaries of the corporation.

■ Stable supply chains form when transaction costs are high relative to the variation in prices over time. The new forms of buying (aggregation, auctions etc.) increase the variability of prices and thus destabilize existing supply chains.

The fact of competition means corporate evolution is an unending process. Over the last thirty years the inexorable pressure to improve has thrown up all sorts of responses to the need to bear down on price and extract maximum value out of the supply chain. Mergers and acquisitions, for example, were designed to cut out volatility by bringing suppliers within the corporate fold. But they too often had the opposite effect by increasing the size of the organization and internal costs.

Then there was widespread enthusiasm for re-engineering to streamline and improve internal functions. It started with simple processes like finance and accounting. But with time and technology it became more ambitious, culminating in the implementation of Electronic Data Interchange to harmonize the interests of parties up and down the supply chain. But the benefits of these efforts, for all their good intention, were too often limited by their creeping universality and by the failure to extend their range much beyond the internal transactions.

Then came the Internet. Web-enabled technology has aggregated demand and vastly improved the flow of information, putting unprecedented downward pressure on external costs and empowering the purchaser. B2B e-commerce, building on the changes that preceded, has seriously destabilized the supply chain and left it vulnerable to the other forces of change building across the business landscape. Forthcoming chapters will explain how corporations will have to respond to this momentous change.

CHAPTER 3

Towards a New-World Context

INTRODUCTION

W E HAVE TOUCHED ON HOW TECHNOLOGY is accelerating corporate change but there are other important forces to consider as well.

The globalization of the production process, for example, has completely overturned the way corporations operate and elevate the concept of brand above price and availability as the key differentiation between comparable goods.

At the same time, consumers have grown immeasurably in sophistication. They have more individualized tastes and are subject to much more complex lifestyle dynamics. The effect has been to place enormous pressure on the corporation to re-orientate itself to survive in this new demand-led environment.

But other major institutions are also feeling the pinch of these changes. Governments need to adapt if they are to be able to fulfill their core competencies in this new age. And again, the pressure looks likely to have a centripetal drive towards fragmentation. We will describe these forces in this chapter to demonstrate how pervasive change is becoming.

TECHNOLOGY – BUILDING A CONNECTED WORLD

Silicon-based technology is one of the most powerful engines driving today's global change. In only twenty-five years since the invention of the silicon chip, more than six billion of the little devices have been embedded into almost every aspect of our social and working lives. IBM foresees a trillion interconnected entities within the next decade, linking people, machines and devices in a continuous electronic web of almost infinite scale.

Stan Davis and Chris Meyer in their book, *Blur*,[1] predicted that the impact of this new connectivity would be greater speed, increased interaction and the rapid rise of intangibles, but it is a historical truism to say that the full effect of technological change is almost never correctly foreseen. When Alexander Graham Bell first demonstrated the telephone to the Mayor of New York, the Major said, "This is an absolutely fascinating device, but what could I possibly do with it?" Bell responded that the telephone would enable the Mayor to talk to people in cities across the entire USA. The Mayor was surprised by Bell's logic. He responded, "Why would I want to do that? I don't know any people in other cities outside New York."

It is not just the speed effects of connectivity that are reshaping new business and social structures. The ability to store, chronicle and recall large amounts of information will have profound effects on the way we live and work. During the time it takes you to read this book, the equivalent of the entire contents of the Encyclopaedia Britannica will have been added to the World Wide Web. The challenge now is to harness the information explosion in a way that is useful and relevant to each one of us.

Nor do we expect the pace of technology-driven innovation to slow down. There are more inventions in the pipeline today than in any period over the last century, in areas extending from biotechnology to material science. From the point of view of communications alone, we are still dipping our toes into the connected world of the fixed line and mobile communications. As we will see in Chapter 4, the advent of visual and virtual communications will enhance electronic interactions by exponential proportions. The only limiting factors are the finite sources of financial and human capital necessary to realize commercial applications. And human rather than financial capital may well be the final limiting factor.

A NEW SOCIAL AGENDA

The production-led economy has fashioned our lives for more than a century. In the jargon of our times, we have created a world of "really good stuff" responding to every permutation of human need. But it has been the producers of "stuff" rather than the recipients that have dictated the speed and direction of this material revolution.

Today, the leading suppliers of consumer products and services can call upon global manufacturing platforms that have been fashioned out of the rationalization, consolidation and re-engineering of local and regional suppliers. These mega-corps produce a constant stream of competitively priced new offerings. And having achieved a global presence, many of these corporations depend entirely on broadcast communication to promote their offerings to consumers. At the heart of such communications lies the brand promise that targets a specific human need or desire such as refreshment. Coca-Cola, for example, one of the acmes of brand philosophy, has made its brand synonymous with the experience of refreshment.

The primary goal of corporations in the nineties was to achieve quantum improvements in operational performance. The process of "re-engineering the corporation," as described in Champy and Hammer's book,[2] sets out to reduce the cost of a product, increase the rate of innovation and improve quality by several factors. For all this change, the end customer carried on largely unaware of these corporate ambitions.

But as the western world becomes saturated with "really good stuff" and the lightning speed of product innovation erodes any prospect of sustained advantage, the consumer is beginning to take center stage. And it promised to be a much more elemental change than anything that happened in the preceding century, when the arrival of the concept of self-service was the most profound reorientation. All that meant ultimately was a wider gap between the consumer and supplier – an alienating phenomenon antithetical to today's change.

FROM SELF-SERVICE TO CO-DEVELOPMENT

In the decade to come, enabled by global connectivity and greater electronic interaction, the relationship between the supplier and the consumer will move away from the self-service model to one of co-development. In the new economy, the customer will become a vital employee of the supplier.

Why should such a dramatic change be necessary? Look at the new generation of teenagers and you will begin to identify the seeds of such change.

In 1987, Nike created a brand based on the slogan "Just do it." The call was for the new generation of teenage consumers to abandon their loyalties to traditional institutions like school and family, and thus become self-determining individuals. In making this powerful statement, Nike connected with a new generation of customer and built one of the world's foremost brand icons.

The success of this brand statement underlies a more fundamental insight. People today are becoming pre-occupied with the quest for personal experience rather than discrete products or services that have been designed for a mass market. Ten percent of university students in the UK now take a gap year before college in the expectation that they can use this time to expand their experience of the world. We can expect the Millennium generation to be more discerning in their attitude towards "stuff" than previous generations that were brought up in an environment weakened by a succession of global conflicts.

Material possessions will naturally remain important to future generations of consumer, but the intangible elements of personal experience will take on greater significance as we become more effective at satisfying the former need. The new social agenda can be summarized in the words – *to be*, *to go*, *to know*, *to do* and *to have fun*. These are experience-based desires and cannot be met simply by new mass products and services. We, as consumers, have woken up to the realization that we are first and foremost individuals governed by personal experiences rather than predictable targets of a corporate marketing campaign.

THE ECONOMICS OF INTELLECTUAL CAPITAL

In a world where competitive advantage can no longer be sustained by product or service innovation, and where the majority of such offers are being rapidly commoditized, the confidence of shareholders in old economy stocks has been substantially undermined.

In the six-month period between September 1999 and February 2000 some of the world's most successful corporations such as Proctor & Gamble saw their shares drop by as much as fifty percentage points (Fig. 3.1).

In response to this resounding vote of no confidence, company executives are looking for new ways of demonstrating shareholder value. At the same time, individuals are revising their patterns of employment and career interests to better exploit new wealth creating opportunities. This is a subject we deal with in much greater detail in Chapters 5 and 6. But let's understand the implications of social and technological change on traditional sources of economic value.

As we illustrated in the previous section, the consumer is taking center stage. The quest for individual experience becomes a major force in the connected economy, and the ability to anticipate such human desires becomes the primary source of value. In the connected economy, it is not so much the transaction itself that produces wealth (that is, the sale of a good or service), but the information that a transaction is about to take place. The airline industry provides a good example of the latter. The profit made on an airline reservation frequently exceeds the margins on air travel itself.

Understanding the customer as a micro market of one becomes the key to unlocking value in the new economy. This is not a skill that the world's largest consumer companies have learnt to master – at least for the moment.

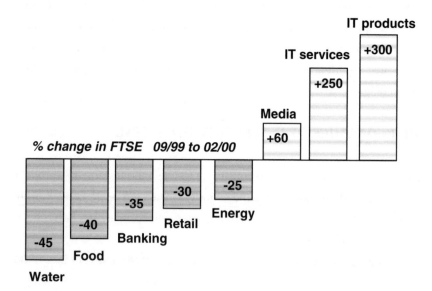

Fig. 3.1 Share price trends of different sectors, 1999–2000.

Travel – valuing the consumer experience

Consider the travel industry. Served largely by mass-market package tour operators, the sector has expanded dramatically through the introduction of low cost offerings aimed at a wider cross-section of the public. Traditionally, the average customer of these packages has often had only a limited experience of travel, and is dependent on suppliers for advice and knowledge. But the emerging generation of consumer is much more sophisticated. Many have traveled extensively through college and seek "out-of-the-ordinary" experiences in place of a two-week break in Florida or Majorca.

The ability of these consumers to search the World Wide Web for attractive new venues and experiences has fueled a successful and growing segment of dot.coms. These corporations, like Travelocity.com and Expedia.com, are focused on air transport and do-it-yourself travel arrangements. We expect to see similar lifestyle Web offerings to emerge in other areas of human activity where personal choice is the core determinant – for example, entertainment, education, and personal well being.

Knowledge of individual customer needs and aspirations will be the new currency that corporations will trade amongst themselves. Such knowledge will become the intellectual capital of many atomized corporations in the new economy and will arise from the relationships that these corporations build and sustain with their customers and trading partners.

At the individual level, the new generations of educated workers will strive not merely for material assets but more for intellectual or intangible ones. Specialized knowledge and experience will command high financial worth and the gap between rich and poor will grow exponentially. Tomorrow's top professionals will have much in common with today's rock stars in terms of exceptional earnings.

POLITICS AND THE POWER OF COMMUNITY

Connectivity will empower the individual but what about its impact on governments and traditional institutions? In a world of almost unfettered mobility and rapid information transfer, governments are struggling to retain control over their citizens and national wealth. As the world virtualizes, capital and knowledge flight becomes a possibility on a grand scale – threatening the power of government to collect taxes and provide core public services for its citizens.

With the increasing mobility of capital and labor, the nation state is eroding in favor of regional power blocks such as the European Economic Union. At the same time, local communities such as towns and cities are becoming ever more influential over our daily lives. In twenty years we predict that nearly three quarters of the world's population will be confined to no more than six hundred cities. This is despite the increasing expense and discomfort of living in a modern metropolis. The city will be the economic and political hub of the new economy. No wonder the positions of Mayor of New York and London are competed for so intensely.

Political differences become less relevant in a connected world. Individual aspiration does not fit so simply into the conventional party political molds. We are witnessing a distinct move to the political center in the world's most advanced economies. Taxes are converging and with them conditions of employment, social welfare and regulation. Globalization has triggered intense competition among governments to provide the most attractive business environment. In this respect, the leading countries are homogenizing.

Because individuals cannot exercise significant political power on their own, communities become the main source of influence over their political masters. And like-minded communities of interest are emerging across the Internet in every sphere of social and political activity. Through collective votes and buying power, these communities become the new source of influence over all corporate bodies. In turn, institutions must learn to engage and harness the power of these nationless communities.

In the face of such powerful defining forces, the birth of the new economy will not be a painless transition. Instead we expect to see exceptional volatility in the world's share markets, the failure of some of the world's largest organizations and more social unrest within the developed countries. Witness the effect of anti-capitalist protests organized over the Internet on political and corporate events. Seattle, Prague, Washington and a growing number of business centers have all experienced this Web-enabled disruption.

In the preceding sections we have described the possible consequences of major forces of change – technical, economic, social and political. Not since the European Renaissance have we witnessed such a comparable period of dramatic development. We are heading towards a new world order, built on universal connectivity. *Our thesis in this book is that such changes will give rise, at an economic level, to a new theory of the firm, and at the business level, to a set of new generic strategies.*

We shall demonstrate here and in subsequent chapters that, at the heart of this new world order, the power of relationships and the importance of information arising from these relationships will become a key lever in defining personal and corporate success.

INFORMATION INTIMACY – INCREASING THE POWER OF RELATIONSHIPS

Information and the relationships it supports are becoming increasingly influential in every aspect of our professional and social lives. Mastering information-based relationships will be the key to unlocking value in the new economy.

Increasingly powerful infrastructures, originating from central mainframes and progressing through to the modern day networked computer are producing meta-changes in the organization and ownership of information across society. With the advent of new multimedia or "intimate" computers, supported by high-speed digital networks, we are about to witness a further quantum change, placing the individual rather than the organization at the center of the emerging information web.

Business and government will need to build a new form of relationship with individual members of society based on anticipation of need and reciprocity of information sharing rather than one-way broadcasts. The individual will recognize these changes as heralding a new era of self-exploration where successful partners will provide a better understanding of personal needs through individualized interactions.

By way of illustration, consider a typical on-line customer relationship with Amazon.com. The bookseller has over two million titles in its on-line catalogue. This gives us almost infinite choice over which book to buy. But the sheer scale of choice becomes more of a problem than an opportunity. There may be fewer than one hundred books within the entire on-line library that we will really feel have changed our lives. But the chance of encountering any one of these is infinitely small.

Amazon.com has set out to profile each individual reader to anticipate new titles that will hit his or her precise interests. As two-way interactions increase between customer and supplier, this may provide some helpful suggestions. However, few of us imagine that it will point the way to the one hundred or less "life-changing" titles. Much work is required to create the necessary levels of intimacy to enable this to happen. Should such logical connections be made, the prize for both reader and book supplier could be remarkably high.

From the past era of information isolation

Until relatively recently, organizations – public and private – held information in central files, where access required the service of professionals such as accountants, recorders and publishers. Personal information was of little importance until a professional had authenticated it.

The advent of the mainframe computer in the sixties reinforced the position of central information systems by providing a similar level of information isolation. Data centers became military installations protected by guards and barbed wire. Central IT departments became the high priests of the information age, enjoying exclusive access to the inner sanctum, the computer room. Even the computer industry itself became heavily centralized with IBM as the dominant influence over hardware, software and standards.

Information isolation was the era of "Them."

Enter the era of information proximity

With the arrival of the mini and personal computers at the end of the seventies, departments began to gain control over their own information by developing applications on local hardware. The mainframe diminished in importance as did its central IT group. Information infrastructures began to fragment as marketing favored Apple computers, engineering favored Compaq and Digital and finance remained loyal to IBM. IT resources dispersed towards the end user, with modest co-ordination from central units. With this information proximity came a new era in which the lay users could exploit computer tools to their own advantage, which meant individuals could begin to take control over their work environments. Suddenly they had tools like desktop publishing to produce high quality publications and reports. The information technology industry itself underwent dramatic changes in the early nineties as the effects of end-user computing reverberated across the world. New entrants such as Microsoft and Compaq began to challenge the incumbents to the point that "Snow White and the seven dwarves" became an endangered species.

Power structures of all kinds have been unsettled by the redistribution of information and computing power. Much of these changes can be linked to information proximity. It has become the era of "Me" rather than "Them."

Towards the new era of information intimacy

We are moving into an era of networks, centered on the global Internet. These networks encourage greater sharing of information between individuals, departments and organizations than was possible even in the era of information proximity. With the advent of more powerful and mobile personal computers, intimate information will be engaged and connected. Interaction will become the primary source of such information, and it will exist only as long as it is needed. With sharing of intimate information we are about to enter the new era of "Us."

The world of information intimacy is interdependent and ephemeral. It constantly shifts and changes according to rules of chaos rather than reason. It builds on relationships between people rather than organization and institutions. It thrives on partnerships, and combines a spirit of co-operation with intense competition. It avoids legal frameworks and national regulatory controls because neither can keep up with the pace of change enabled by interconnected information webs – witness the effect of Napster on the music industry and the convoluted and protracted legal response. The individual rather than the organization or nation state becomes the controlling influence in the forth-coming information economy.

STRUCTURES BASED ON RELATIONSHIPS

With improved connectivity and the associated transparency of information, economic power moves away from the corporation, especially those that are internally-focused, towards key external relationships. As we have seen in this chapter, customer choice becomes a determining economic force in the trans-action of goods and services. The concept of mass markets diminishes in favor of markets-of-one, responding directly to individual need. But it is not only the customer relationship that will generate value in the new economy. A corpora-tion has relationships with a multiplicity of stakeholders – the customer being an important but non-exclusive stakeholder.

And the relationships with all stakeholders will be the central links of the extended organization upon which our atomized economy will be constructed.

Instead of being product or service centric, tomorrow's corporations will be relationship centric. The nature of business will be focused on extracting value from each relationship through constant interactions and information sharing.

SUMMARY

Technological, social, economic and political change, all interrelated, have converged to produce a whirlwind that is ripping through established struc-tures. Nothing is untouched. The effect is towards atomization and the evolu-tion of smaller units better equipped to deal with the pace of change and the demands of consumers, whether on the high street or in the polling booth.

And not only are these essential components of the business environ-ment and the social economy changing but their interactions are being rede-fined. There is a growing sensitivity to the importance of these relationships, which will be the key to unlocking the potential of the new economy. It is about understanding and leveraging the individualized information that is produced by intimate exchanges.

The challenge for governments will be to work out how to cope with the new alignments that threaten to erode their traditional competences. Corporations, meanwhile, will have to find ways of mining the value of their myriad relationships, both with customers and with their other stakeholders, and determine how much of their traditional functions they can try to perform without becoming dangerously unwieldy.

CHAPTER 4

A Revolution in Digital Connectivity

INTRODUCTION

W E ARE ALL FAMILIAR with the electrifying pace at which the technology we use has developed in recent years. No sooner have you become comfortable with a piece of software or a digital device than something new arrives to take its place. But something more dramatic is set to happen in the years ahead. It will be more than just the addition of a few new bells and whistles. It will be a massive broadening of the communications media away from simply text or voice-based media to the visual and the virtual.

The revolution has only just begun. This chapter will discuss how this advance will manifest itself – whether it be something from the pages of Arthur C. Clarke or Gameboys-with-attitude. And we will speculate about the impact these new interfaces will have on existing relationships and how they will affect the structure of the corporation of the future.

A QUANTUM STEP IN PERSONAL COMMUNICATIONS

Electronic devices are the individual's link with the information world. From the traditional rotary phone operated by the network utility in the fifties to the wide range of personal communicators and computers of the current decade, we are witnessing a revolution in device mobility and versatility. In turn, we are facing imminent danger of information and communications overload.

Of greatest consequence to the individual in recent years has been the mobile phone and the personal digital assistant (or PDA). Facilitated by common standards and fierce competition amongst operators, the mobile phone has exceeded all expectations in rates of adoption across the world. It is now a consumer device enjoyed by hundreds of millions of business and domestic users and in some countries such as Finland, Sweden and Japan exceeds fixed-phone populations.

At the same time, hand-held personal digital assistants, PDAs, are proliferating in number and capability, from the early Psion Organiser and the Palm Pilot to the Windows CE devices of Compaq and Hewlett-Packard. Such devices enable pen-based writing input, and can store personal information such as contacts, diaries and e-mails.

The emerging Universal Mobile Telecommunications System (UMTS) will enable such mobile devices to interconnect via high-speed digital links using whatever radio system is available, from in-building micro-cells to global satellite links. Already, integrated PDA/telephones are appearing from leading mobile phone suppliers such as Nokia and Ericsson. But the lack of compelling applications, combined with poor ergonomics, have limited market success to date. New generations of product from both PDA and mobile phone suppliers look likely to overcome such initial shortcomings.

New technologies and standards such as Blue Tooth for personal wireless networks connecting a wide range of appliances may offer further scope for device-to-device connectivity. It is possible today to connect a digital music player (MP3 device) with a personal digital assistant, mobile phone and lap top computer using a personal wireless network. This gives complete mobility around the house, office or other social setting. Car manufacturers are developing networks within the motor vehicle that will interconnect a variety of business and entertainment devices to external wireless networks. John Chambers, CEO of Cisco, has spoken recently of his own corporation's plans to help wire up the home, with Internet connections reaching every domestic electronics device.

The prospect of a trillion connected devices looks alarmingly real, as UMTS standards bodies debate whether each individual on the planet should have either one thousand or one million unique addresses to reference the many devices that will support our lives. The vast increase in personal communications will occur once such issues are agreed internationally, and appliance manufacturers can embed communicating devices into every aspect of our domestic and working lives.

A NEW GENERATION OF MEDIA PROCESSOR

One of the main limitations to personal communications today is the personal computer itself. Current generations of microprocessors are sophisticated data and text handlers, but relatively underpowered in their image and video processing capabilities. At least three years of price performance improvement is needed to enable low-cost home devices to take on full two-way image handling capabilities, including image capture, cataloguing, storage and retrieval. Additional advances in software are also required to handle the complexity of image processing.

We predict that by 2005 an entirely new generation of personal computer, or media processor, will be available on the market with the following characteristics:

- high quality flat screen able to display both television and two-way multimedia information;
- speech, digital camera and pen-based input, and optional touch-screen keyboard;
- full telephone, messaging and interactive video communication through fixed and wireless networks;
- networked and stand-alone processing capabilities, with smart card actuation, and full multimedia features; and
- "always-on" feature that receives and sends out information even when the user is not interacting with the device.

Using personal software agents, the media processor will be able to carry out active negotiation on behalf of its owner, finding useful and relevant information from the increasing number of digital information sources and communications channels. Sometimes the negotiation will involve payment, sometimes a security check. Privacy will become a key feature to overcome the problems of information overload. Over time the media processor will be able to learn about its owner's preferences, and actively provide him or her with a relevant diet of entertainment, information, education and home shopping offers.

This is where Alan Kay's "intimate computer" enters the picture, as the successor to the mainframe of the 1960s and 1970s and the personal computer of the 1980s and 1990s. Mobility will be a primary requirement for such a device as it offers its users physical freedom to work and relax wherever and whenever. As the boundaries between the workplace, home and social setting begin to dissolve; the intimate computer will provide the single point of media access to support all these activities. Such devices will come in all shapes and sizes, from wall-mounted screens to wearable accessories. Wristwatch communicators are already on sale in Japan. Giant living-room and conference-room displays that can be hung on the wall will be available in the next two years at realistic prices.

But however powerful these media processes become, they are limited in use without multimedia networks to support them. The rollout of high-speed digital switched networks – both fixed line and mobile – is a key priority for most telephone operators today. We anticipate a staged approach, taking us from today's predominantly verbal networks to tomorrow's visual and virtual networks.

THE IMPENDING VERBAL–VISUAL–VIRTUAL REVOLUTION

Digital network developments will extend the reach and richness of communications through three distinct eras – verbal, visual and virtual. Each era promises a set of innovations that will transform the way we use communications in our work and domestic lives (Fig. 4.1).

Underlying the verbal–visual–virtual revolution is the proliferation of transmission and switching systems that are competing to provide low-cost, broadband communications. Most nations are liberalizing their telecommunications markets to encourage investment in alternative network infrastructures. Coax and fiber-optic cable systems are competing with twisted-pair copper wire to support telephony traffic as well as Internet and TV. Radio, or wireless, networks are competing with fixed networks to support voice and data traffic over the airwaves.

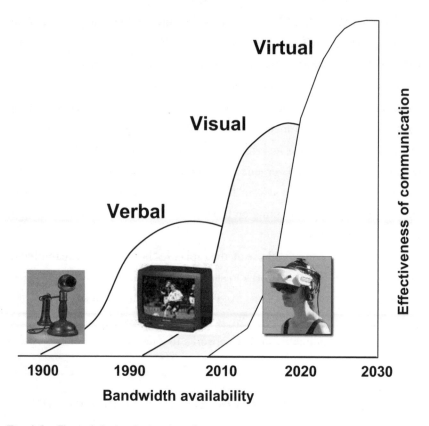

Fig. 4.1 The verbal–visual–virtual revolution.

Extending the verbal era

The spoken and written word has been the principal means of communication through history. The last century saw a massive leap forward in the range of potential modes of communication but it remained chiefly verbal. Telephony has made significant inroads into traditional forms of written communication, for instance in the home-shopping sector where telephone-based transactions have almost entirely replaced postal order forms. And today, in some parts of the world, e-mail services have largely superseded facsimile and postal mail.

Four voice- and text-based technologies promise to boost verbal communication's efficiency and effectiveness over the next five years. These include:

■ *digital cellular telephony* based on second and third generation mobile standards will enable people to communicate voice and non-voice (data, text and image) traffic from any country using a universal terminal device;

■ *new software agents* or personal mediators will enable communications devices to actively filter the flood of voice- and text-based communications traffic to the office or home;

■ *speech recognition* will enable accurate interpretation of natural language input directly from the telephone thus reducing the need for operator assisted services; and

■ *speech translation* over the telephone will enable simultaneous translation to take place between a multiplicity of languages such as English and Chinese in real time.

These developments will continue to sustain speech and text as the primary communications medium supporting commercial interactions between customers and commercial organizations. Just look at how radically the telephone has transformed the insurance sector in the UK by promoting direct sales of insurance products. And speech recognition could transform financial services as customers gain direct access to their investments without human assistance.

The rapid development of the Internet over the last five years has accelerated text-based communications. The ubiquity of the personal computer in the office and home and the availability of universal standards are creating a global network infrastructure within which e-mail messages can be exchanged, and information of all kinds retrieved. The Internet has become the primary platform for electronic commerce and associated home shopping and electronic banking applications. Its extension into the mobile domain with WAP and I-Mode standards will continue to enhance its importance as a text-based information and transaction medium.

Towards the visual era

Although one-way video broadcasting has been with us for over fifty years, two-way visual communications remains in its infancy. But the growing sophistication of personal computers combined with broadband transmission and switching techniques is bringing us close to a critical transition point in the development of visual communications.

The visual era promises improvements in the quality and richness of personal communications that far out-strip those of the verbal era – "a picture is worth a thousand words." The advances in two-way visual communication will be analogous to the transition from radio to TV in the entertainment world, and the effects will be as far reaching. The range of service capabilities becoming available in the visual world include the following.

- *Multimedia kiosks* that combine interactive visual displays, speech input and videoconference links to remote locations. These kiosks already provide unmanned branches for banking, travel and retail services in the high street, and could transition into the home environment as a domestic electronic commerce outlet and multimedia center.
- *Desktop videoconferencing* that enables remote parties to see as well as hear each other, and to share visual information. Such systems have been in commercial use for some years, but the advent of digital cameras, multimedia personal computers, signal compression techniques and ISDN links (both fixed and mobile) will accelerate adoption as costs tumble.
- *Interactive TV* linking people to powerful video servers over broadband networks is being rolled out over cable and telephone networks. Early applications include video-on-demand, electronic banking and home shopping. Already millions of consumers in the UK are linked via such devices in the OPEN service.

The most likely stimulus for the visual era will be video-streaming developments on the World Wide Web. A growing number of Web sites contain video materials, and with the aid of digital cameras, any individual can create his or her own home broadcast studio. In the same way that desktop publishing brought down the barriers for small business enterprises to enter various information-based markets, so video Web sites have already and will continue to encourage new entrants to emerge in the entertainment and broadcast sector.

Surpassing reality – into the virtual era

The virtual era promises extraordinary new communications services such as Tele-presence and Tele-robotics that could extend communications way beyond where we are today. Virtual reality (VR) techniques, some of which are already practicable, will dramatically augment communications by providing three-dimensional images of scenes and objects. The potential in the entertainment field is most obvious in electronic gaming. Video gamers will meet in cyber cafes, at home, and ultimately in the electronic ether, to conduct global leisure wars in three dimensions.

Beyond Tele-entertainment lies virtual conferencing in which participants wearing VR headsets can link into a virtual conference room to explore computer generated artifacts that can range from a white board to a three-dimensional product prototype. In the engineering sector, the concept of a virtual design team is already well established. Such virtual conference tools could enhance the effectiveness of such teams by integrating CAD/CAM and computer simulation modeling into a shared workspace.

Tele-presence is another virtual communications technology. With Tele-presence, stereoscopic vision and mechanical movement are transmitted between remote locations, enabling one person to be virtually in two places at the same time. Tele-surgery is a recent innovation that enables a surgeon to conduct a remote operation on a patient by using stereoscopic vision to examine the patient, and Tele-robotics to carry out the mechanics of the operation. Using new techniques, the surgeon can now experience full tactile feedback from the patient, giving a true-to-life experience.

Because virtual technologies are digital, they are also scaleable, which opens the door to a host of new applications. Tele-surgery, for example, could be applied to microscopic situations where miniature robots perform micro-surgery.

MEETING THE COST OF A CONNECTED WORLD

Within the next ten years, business and domestic customers will benefit enormously from the increased reach and capability of digital networks. But just as railroad construction in the nineteenth century required investors with deep pockets, so too will the continuous improvement of global telecommunications networks – taking us beyond today's verbal capabilities into the visual and virtual eras. In the case of the railroads, few early investors realized economic returns, a fact that is not entirely lost on today's investment institutions.

Having climbed in the nineties to the pinnacle of stock market acclamation, many of the world's leading telecommunications operators have fallen recently out of favor with investors – thus denying them of much needed investment funds. The reasons include the rapid commoditization of current services combined with the growing cost of building enhanced (e.g. high-speed digital) networks.

With intense competition taking place between fixed line (twisted pair and cable) and wireless operators (mobile phone and satellite), telephony and Internet services are already becoming low cost commodities. Although this is in the customer's short-term favor, it reduces operator capacity for re-investment in new network services. Current pricing trends suggest that time and distance independent tariffs will emerge within the next two years for all but the most sophisticated services (such as high-quality video conferencing).

With the recent auctions for third generation mobile networks, the telecommunications sector has taken a trillion-dollar gamble into new multimedia services with as yet few proven applications. To compound difficulties, many governments have chosen to divert their multi-billion dollar license fee windfalls away from the telecommunications sector into other unrelated areas. Given the growing importance of universal high-speed connectivity to national competitive advantage, one has to question the wisdom of such actions. In our opinion, a modest proportion of the twenty-two billion pounds of license income in the UK would have been well spent underwriting the deployment of fiber optic cable to every business and home in the country.

The combination of the threat to future profit flows from existing services such as telephony, and uncertainty over the viability of new network services such as third generation mobile has dampened investor confidence in the telecommunications sector. In particular, the debt burden that was the by-product of the gamble over third generation licenses may be enough to deflate the entire information technology sector in the coming years if operators fail to achieve early returns from these unparalleled investments. As always, winning applications and subsequent funding will be necessary to ensure that we all benefit from the fruits of the digital age.

SUMMARY

Yet again, it is the individual that will be most conspicuously empowered by this revolution in digital connectivity, taking us beyond simply verbal communication to more visual and virtual media. The ease with which the "connected" can access vast quantities of information has already been and will grow ever liberating in the workplace and the home.

But someone has to pick up the tab for the monumental technological investment that is a prerequisite for all this. And it won't just be a one-off cost like laying a railway network. It is going to need constant upgrading, perhaps as frequently as at five-year intervals at the cost of trillions of dollars each time around.

The investor's appetite is already delicate. Witness the performance of technology markets during 2000–2001, where confidence was devastated not just by a realization that a lot of the emerging companies were at best unsustainable and sometimes downright silly. New technical capabilities will have to show much more tangible benefits if they are to get the money they need to establish themselves. And that, in itself, will be yet another force for change on the corporate landscape.

However, someone must pay for these dramatic innovations in communications capability. It is not merely a matter of building the industrial railroad a second time, but more a matter of upgrading such facilities on a five-yearly basis at a cost of a trillion dollars a time. As we are witnessing in the case of third generation mobile telephones, the investor appetite for innovation is at best finite. New technical capabilities will need to demonstrate tangible economic benefit both to suppliers and customers, as each will be expected to contribute ultimately to the financial costs.

PART III
Drivers

So far, we have talked about external pressures on the corporation – empowered consumers, changing technology and new economic pressures. But it's not just push – the corporation will *want* to change.

Why? Because both "old" and "new" economy shares are taking a pasting on the markets, so where can the CEO go? The assets are already sweating, and the only new sources of value are current relationships and knowledge assets. But these new sources of value are unlocked by agility, so new wealth must mean new corporate structures.

CHAPTER 5

New Sources of
Shareholder Wealth

INTRODUCTION

S O FAR, WE HAVE REVIEWED the factors which make atomization possible –
changes in business economics, changes in consumer behavior and changes
in technology. We have not yet looked at the drivers that we think make atomization inevitable – the need to provide new sources of wealth for shareholders.

The invention of the microprocessor has been one of the most important
driving forces behind the huge increase of the world's stock markets since the
1970s. The connected economy stocks in particular have facilitated an unparalleled creation of new wealth. But the first year of the new millennium marked
an important stage in that process, with a devastating reappraisal of corporate
value concluding a brief period of hysterical investment patterns.

This chapter will look at how this latest stage in the ongoing technological revolution has raised a new level of expectation about company performance, in both the new and old sectors of the economy. The clumsy differentiation between the two constituents, that was for a time underpinned by
contradictory rationales, has been at least partially reconciled. We will propose our own formula to marry the two that presages the desirability of widespread corporate restructuring in the future.

ESCAPING FROM THE FUNDAMENTALS

Many of the most successful twentieth-century investors such as Warren
Buffett have selected their stock portfolios based on those corporations offering strong future profit flows from well established businesses, backed by solid
assets. These were not merely limited to manufacturers of products but also
service corporations operating in the traditional publishing, insurance and fi-

nancial sectors where prudent management ensured healthy cash flows and strong returns. The same investors have chosen to stay well away from the high-tech corporations who have enjoyed a meteoric rise associated with the connected economy. Were they wise to ignore some of the most remarkable growth opportunities of all time?

Based on recent work of Cap Gemini Ernst & Young's Center for Business Innovation (see *Net Future Expectations* box below), these cautious investors were half right and half wrong. A simple expression of shareholder wealth developed and tested by the Center suggests that in the current volatile markets, shareholder wealth is defined as the sum of two equally significant components.

The first component is the net present value of all future profit flows generated by today's established business operations; that is, those units that address established market needs with sustainable products and services. Such businesses form the corner stone of Warren Buffett's investment criteria. The second and equally important component of shareholder wealth is the projected profits of all future growth opportunities where significant investment and experimentation is being committed by management. This contrasts with the actual generators of income for the shareholders, the current profitability of the corporation.

Taken together, these two factors suggest a balance between the here and now and "jam" tomorrow (Fig. 5.1). Any corporation that focuses exclusively on current profitability and associated cost cutting measures will incur substantial market discounts of up to 50 percent – as has been demonstrated in recent stock market revaluations of old economy corporations. Equally, those corporations that have never shown a profit and are negative cash generators are also being discounted heavily, as the fall in NASDAQ in 2001 suggests.

NET FUTURE EXPECTATIONS

Net Future Expectations (NFE) is CAP Gemini Ernst & Young's approach to valuing new economy businesses. It takes into account both current and future value drivers and builds on traditional valuation methods in an innovative way. The inadequacies of standard valuation tools are well rehearsed and we do not need to reiterate them here, but suffice it to say that NFE provides a framework

---

for understanding why certain new economy businesses are valued at more than they are apparently worth.

NFE as a concept is based on the fact that new ways of doing business have created a whole new set of intangible assets that do not show up in any of the traditional yardsticks such as ROI or DCF. Put simply, the formula goes:

Net Future Expectations = Discounted Cash Flow + Net Future Opportunity

It is the Net Future Opportunity (NFO) element that has previously confounded analysts and which is the key to understanding the real value in new economy businesses. It is comprised mainly of the "intangible" assets of a company, and notwithstanding the confusion surrounding the issue, these assets are readily quantifiable. CGEY discovered that the NFO of a business is made up three parts:

- its capacity for innovation,
- the flexibility with which it is able to adapt to changes in the marketplace, and
- its ability to execute a given strategy.

A corporation's capacity for innovation can best be understood in terms of its R&D leadership, its technological expertise and its ability to quickly deliver new products and platforms to a market with ever changing needs. It can be measured by assessing among other things the corporation's R&D spend, new product pipeline and cycle times and intellectual property portfolio. Similarly a corporation's flexibility can be quantified by (for example) the percent of revenue which comes from new products and services each year, its number of strategic partnerships and its cost of capital. Executional ability is evidenced in a corporation's market share, customer satisfaction and retention scores and brand value.

Shareholder value =	NPV of existing business model	+	Future growth options
Uncertainty	• Low		• High
Performance indicators	• Lagging • Financial		• Leading • Non-financial
Key drivers & intangibles	• Efficiency • Current products & related brands		• Innovation • Flexibility • Ability to execute
Tools & techniques	• DCF/ EVA/ROI		• Real option frameworks e.g. decision trees, simulation etc.

With kind permission from Ernst & Young

Fig. 5.1 Share value includes intangible elements.

This balanced view of shareholder wealth helps to explain the historic stock market rise of silicon-based corporations, where a healthy combination of profits and future growth opportunities have been the norm. However, the formula falls short of defining the main factors that contribute to sustained value in the new economy. To construct a useful analytical tool, further elaboration of competitive forces is necessary, as we shall see in the next chapter.

The impact of this equation can be measured by looking at the correlation between market capitalization, earnings, dividends paid and market sentiment (as expressed by P/E ratio) of a basket of new and old economy corporations – see Fig. 5.2. While the figures presented are based on corporate valuations in May 2001, analysis shows that the implications are consistent over time.

The valuations show that there is a reasonable correlation between earnings and dividends paid (as you would expect). But, they also show a large negative correlation between dividend paid and P/E ratio. Profits in the new economy appear to be inversely proportional to market sentiment – or to put it in English, if you return good profits to your owners, you can expect the value of your shares to remain low!

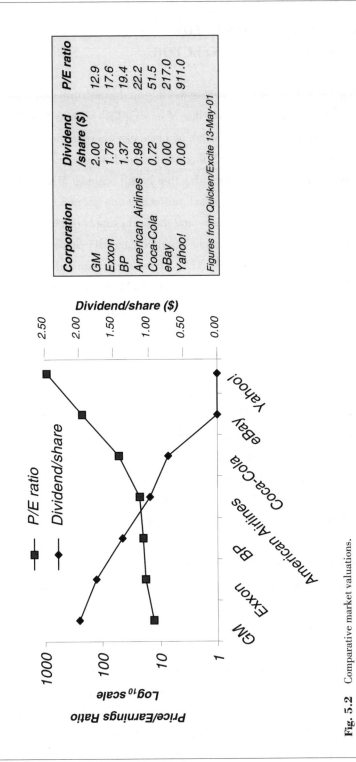

Corporation	Dividend /share ($)	P/E ratio
GM	2.00	12.9
Exxon	1.76	17.6
BP	1.37	19.4
American Airlines	0.98	22.2
Coca-Cola	0.72	51.5
eBay	0.00	217.0
Yahoo!	0.00	911.0

Figures from Quicken/Excite 13-May-01

Fig. 5.2 Comparative market valuations.

A QUIET REVOLUTION IN THE TELECOMMUNICATIONS SECTOR

Although the big news of the seventies was the rapid growth in mainframe computer sales and the associated rise in value of its suppliers such as IBM, Burroughs, and CDC, a quiet revolution was taking place elsewhere in the telecommunications sector. Here, the infusion of silicon into a largely electro-mechanical product industry caused a major restructuring that is still ongoing. Many of the world's largest telecommunications manufacturers of that time are no longer in business – like Western Electric and Plessey – and the world supply of telecommunications equipment has shrunk from over one-hundred national manufacturers to just six global suppliers – Alcatel, Nortel, NEC, Siemens, Ericsson and Lucent.

The effect of silicon on the industry has been felt in two ways. Firstly it transformed the means of manufacture and equipment support by reducing labor-intensive tasks. This led to dramatic downsizing of both suppliers and telecommunications operators – often to the frustration and confusion of their public sector owners. Privatization became the effective remedy to pass this problem from public to private sector hands. The second effect was the rapid innovation of features and facilities introduced by computer control and digital switching. This accelerated the opportunities for network innovation and associated investment capital. Only the largest suppliers and operators were able to generate sufficient R&D funds to invest in next generation digital networks – leading to rapid global consolidation of players across the sector.

More recently, the convergence of multimedia communications through more sophisticated digital switching and fiber-based transmission systems has further accelerated development within the sector. New players operating fiber networks have been financed to compete with inefficient public operators left over from the state monopoly days. Other players such as Cisco have emerged to satisfy the vast demand for data related switching and transmission equipment – the so-called "plumbing of the Internet."

Now attention has turned to ownership of the local network, or the last mile, to businesses and homes. Cable has taken on a high premium due to its ability to bypass traditional channels such as the telephone connection. The equity premium commanded by many cable franchises illustrates the power of future growth options. Recent cable corporation transactions indicate an equity value of $3–5000 for each home passed by the cable. Less than half of this relates to the current business of providing a bundle of TV channels and basic telephony services. The rest is based on the potential value of future digital services such as electronic commerce, device-to-device communications and new broadband applications such as webcams (Fig. 5.3).

With the silicon regeneration of the telecommunications sector, investor sentiment has been bullish for well over a decade. Until recently, manufacturers such as Cisco, Nortel and Lucent have provided shareholders with spectacular returns as have many of the privatized carriers and cable operators such as TCI, Deutsche Telecom and France Telecom. However a new sense of reality is beginning to hit the market with the advent of third generation mobile. This may be just enough to cause a stock market implosion reaching well beyond the boundaries of the telecommunications sector and causing a temporary slow down of the entire connected economy.

FUNDING THE NEW ECONOMY'S RAILROADS

The analogy with the railroads of the industrial revolution has been used many times to moderate investors' expectations. Few, if any, railroad investors made

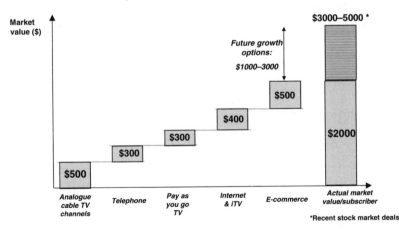

Fig. 5.3 Derivation of stock market valuations of cable businesses (per subscriber).

sustainable profits from these new means of transport, and today most modern railways are operated as loss-making utilities within the public sector. However, analysts would argue that in a connected economy, a growing proportion of goods and services will be transacted through electronic channels, and thus network operators should find ways of benefiting from this trade.

This has never been the case with any other type of transport system, and is unlikely to be so for telecommunications unless the operator has influence on or control over the transactions themselves. Looking at the complete on-line supply chain, this means that telecommunications carriers will need to participate well beyond the boundaries of "network operations" into areas such as content navigation and content provision (Fig. 5.4). Note the interest of many such operators in becoming Internet Service Providers (ISPs).

However, despite the poor prospects of gaining economic returns, the relentless demand for improved transmission continues as we embrace the new visual and virtual eras of communication. What we are seeing today is that to build the truly connected economy, we will have to progressively upgrade the infrastructure from today's low-speed copper pipes to tomorrow's high-speed fiber optic and wireless circuits. This is equivalent to a complete renewal of the railroad system every five to ten years!

With the recent auctioning of third generation mobile licenses – designed to enable a multimedia version of the highly popular, telephony-based mobile communications service – the cost of transportation begins to look unobtainably high. Given that this trillion-dollar-plus investment is just one of many new channel options being invested in, the stock markets are becoming jus-

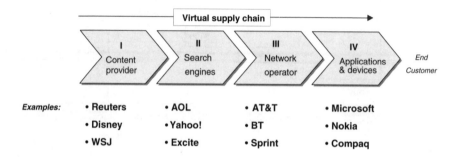

Fig. 5.4   The new economy on-line supply chain.

tifiably concerned about the likely returns on capital employed. The recent deterioration of telecommunications stocks will continue until suppliers and operators can demonstrate two baseline conditions.

The first is that the new multimedia highways fulfill concrete needs for business and domestic purposes. We can all envision exciting new mobile applications that provide us with information on the fly, but who will sponsor these applications from concept through to widespread commercial services, and will the customer be willing to pay the premium prices associated with the new technologies?

The second condition is that network operators will be able to extract adequate economic value from the new services. With growing competition amongst operators and different modes of transport (e.g. cable, satellite, twisted pair) the market for basic connectivity is fast commoditizing. A diminishing proportion of revenue is available for reinvestment in new network capabilities implying that rapid industry consolidation must take place to ensure that innovation can be funded.

To generate adequate returns on capital employed, the pricing of telecommunications services will need to evolve from today's line-minute basis of charging to a measure relating more directly to the economic value of the connection itself (see Fig. 5.5). In the area of electronic commerce, for example, this corresponds to a proportion of the money transfer and the associated information about the nature of the transaction itself. The latter will become increasingly valuable as it helps to profile an individual's preferences and thus improves promotional campaigns and customized offers. As we shall see in the next chapter, it becomes the prime component of relational capital.

Applying our current view of shareholder wealth to a telecommunications carrier such as British Telecom or AT&T, the rapid commoditization of today's primary services – telephony and Internet traffic – will have the effect of diminishing the net present value of profits from current business operations. The component reflecting future growth options becomes progressively less attractive as the high cost of network redevelopment is set against uncertain new multi-media revenue predictions.

The recent stock market response is to discount substantially global leaders in the carrier sector and thus increase the effective cost of capital for

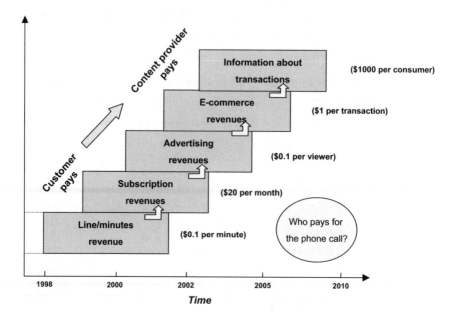

Fig. 5.5   Network income trends (from line-minutes to transaction percentages).

new network projects. In turn, the telecommunications supply sector has seen its own value eroded by diminishing prospects for infrastructural renewal, especially at the pace anticipated by new-economy pundits.

FROM CARBON TO SILICON

The revolution in telecommunications is just one example of how silicon has been transforming the global economy. The application of information technology to every aspect of our industrial structure has brought progressive and ever shorter wavelengths of change. Such has been the success of the information technology industry that its leaders have gained a near monopoly within the top fifty of the world's most valuable corporations. The main losers have been the oil companies who despite continuing profit growth have failed to demonstrate compelling future growth opportunities (Fig. 5.6).

The promise to investors of the information technology sector has been a unique combination of high profitability and rapid growth. During the eighties,

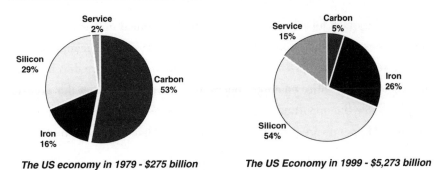

The US economy in 1979 - $275 billion　　　**The US Economy in 1999 - $5,273 billion**

Figures are for top 25 companies in the US economy at year end 1979 and 1999.

Silicon-based industries include IT hardware, software and Internet-based companies.
Carbon-based industries are primarily oil, gas and chemical.
Iron-based industries are traditional industrial manufacturers.
Service companies are primarily in the financial services sector.

Fig. 5.6　Comparison of market values, 1979 and 2000.

for example, the industry achieved a compound rate of 30 percent growth and double-digit profits. This led to stock market valuations based on spectacular earnings multiples. In 1999, Microsoft achieved a market value five times greater than General Motors despite having revenues of just one fifth that of the world's largest car manufacturer.

The success of the information technology industry and its high rate of growth have depended entirely on the ability of its customers to find productive applications for new products and services. In the early phases of computing, these applications were limited largely to financial management and accounting within large corporations. Today they extend to every aspect of a business, whether large or small, and have automated entire supply chains. They also extend to the domestic domain, from computer games to home management systems.

The barometer of the information technology industry continues to be the rate of growth of the IT budget within major corporations. During times of recession, such as the early nineties, IT budgets were frozen. This created a flattening in market demand, and a subsequent drop in the valuation of key computer suppliers such as IBM. Some of these recessionary effects were mitigated by growth in new services such as business re-engineering – designed to help corporations cope with poor economic conditions. However, the beneficiaries here were mainly the service companies who had little direct connection with product.

As the quest for new avenues of growth continued during the eighties and nineties, IT corporations began to move away from their manufacturing roots towards broader business services, ranging from software development to outsourcing of entire computer operations. By embarking on this course, suppliers saw the opportunity to generate revenues well in excess of direct corporate IT spend – frequently as low as one percent of revenue in traditional sectors.

Fuelled by the endless need to meet stock market expectations for growth, many of these corporations are looking to take on wider outsourcing activities encompassing the entire back-office processes of a corporation. In the recent language of Hewlett-Packard, these are referred to as e-services.

It may well be argued that the transfer of these non-core activities to a third party can benefit a large corporation by simplifying the scope of its management responsibilities. However, the recipients of these non-core activities seem to benefit disproportionately in terms of their subsequent stock market valuations.

In simple terms, *outsourcing has become a transfer of wealth from old economy to new economy stocks*.

Despite the growing stock market discrepancies between the traditional industries and its new IT counterparts, a spirit of partnership has persisted up to recent times.

ENTER THE DOT.COM ERA

With a seasoned eye for new growth opportunities, it was not long before analysts began to lock on to the spectacular take-up of the Internet. Figures during the mid-nineties showed monthly growth rates of 15 percent for Internet users. With these came wild speculation that the majority of retail trade would migrate to electronic channels by early in the twenty-first century and new businesses on the Web would be able to attract hundreds of millions of consumers. Many large organizations believed that they were likely to be eradicated by agile Silicon-valley based start-ups that could exploit Internet-based business models to change the rules of doing business, the so-called "destroy.coms."

The stock market take-off point for the new era was the successful flotation of Netscape by Jim Clarke. Netscape was a start-up corporation offering network browser software for personal computers connected to the Internet. Netscape chose to give the early software versions away to establish a large installed base of Internet users. It was so successful that Netscape created a *de facto* standard that challenged Microsoft's dominant industry position.

One of Netscape's most striking achievements was to conduct an Initial Public Offering (IPO) on NASDAQ of over one billion dollars without having made a dime of profit in its short lifetime. In effect, it tipped the balance of shareholder wealth away from current profits towards future possibilities thereby unleashing the vast quantities of investment funds that were needed to fuel the Internet boom.

The result was an unparalleled flight of human and financial capital into the new economy – in search of a frenetic land grab. The entry ticket to become a successful dot.com player was a financing package large enough to buy one's way onto the World Wide Web. This consisted of a top management team (incentivized by sky-high stock options), a robust Web site and supporting business system able to handle millions of transactions per day, supplier partnerships, and enough advertising budget to let the world know you were in business. In the rush of initial players, few were able to assess the real cost of acquiring a critical mass of stable customers – often measured in thousands of dollars. The effect of the new gold rush was an outflow of many billions of dollars of venture capital into highly speculative territory, largely focused on business-to-consumer applications. The beneficiaries were the equipment and network service suppliers as well as the consultants, accountants, lawyers and advertising agencies required to plan and launch the ventures. After an avalanche of sky-high initial public offerings, investors began to apply caution – recognizing that the large majority of new dot.coms offered little or no prospects of early profit flows. Again, the simple application of our shareholder wealth formula showed that value is generated by a combination of current profits and future possibilities. Only the most successful businesses of the new era such as AOL, Amazon and Yahoo! could show any possibility of future profit flows.

Following the dramatic re-adjustment of the markets in early 2000, much needed investment capital has run scared, thus endangering many new

NETSCAPE

Netscape's "Navigator" browser software is the David to Microsoft's "Explorer" Goliath. One of the most successful start-ups of the last seven years, Netscape came not only to challenge the strategic direction of the incumbent software giant, it was the phenomenon that kicked off the whole dot.com boom-and-bust cycle.

Netscape had relatively humble beginnings in a software program called Mosaic, which was developed at the University of Illinois-Champign's National Center for Supercomputer Applications (NCSA). In April 1994, Marc Andreesen and several other NCSA developers left the University and joined with Jim Clark, founder of Silicon Graphics to form Netscape Communications Corp. Their aim was to build on the work done with Mosaic to create a simple graphical way of viewing the then unsophisticated Internet. And they did.

When Netscape went public in 1995, it was one of the first and most highly-publicized Internet IPOs, not least because it was yet to make a profit. And these were the days when an IPO without a profit was a highly innovative concept.

Despite this, demand for Netscape stock was so high that the company increased the initial offering from 3.5m shares to 5m and then upped the price from $14 to $28. The share price rose to $75 on offer day before closing at $58.25. It eventually hit $174 before a two-for-one split in 1996. The hype surrounding it was enormous: Andreesen became a media star adorning the cover of *Time* magazine in his bare feet. James Breyer of the Venture Capital firm Accel Partners claimed: "it's nosebleed valuation, but there's no competitor like it."

That was until Microsoft woke up. Netscape's software forced Microsoft, until then the undisputed king of computer software, to revise totally its strategy and embrace the Internet. It was Microsoft's response to the Netscape Navigator that led to the software giant being prosecuted under US anti-trust laws.

Netscape helps to shore up our NFE thinking – i.e. valuation heavily in the future bucket. It was also one of the first IPOs without profit.

Despite losing market share, Netscape, now under the umbrella of AOL Time Warner, is still the main competition to Microsoft's "Explorer" and is steadily building alternative revenue streams.

start-ups that need second round financing to achieve critical mass. The casualties have been numerous and have swung attention back to the traditional economy corporations.

We think the connected economy offers excellent opportunities to create new ways of doing business based on the Internet and other interactive communications channels. But the dot.com boom-and-bust cycle illustrates that this will take much more than pure human and financial capital to achieve. We maintain that the missing ingredient for success is established relationships. As we shall demonstrate in Chapter 6, this is an area where old-economy companies have much to offer over their new-economy counterparts.

SUMMARY

Shareholders are no longer content with traditional valuations but want a company to demonstrate its preparedness for future developments. The market's rough treatment of long-time strong performers has made that painfully clear. But nowhere is the present conundrum clearer than in the telecoms sector, where technological advances have been more pronounced and have already had such a giant impact on the structure of the industry.

The relentless demand for investment to keep pace with technological progress has scared investors, who have accordingly discounted many of the big players. Some of this can be blamed on an overreaction to the fallacies of the dot.com era. The fallout just reinforced the need to combine traditional valuation techniques, not least some respect for old-fashioned profit making, with demonstrable future promise.

But it doesn't alter the likely impact of the resulting change to the financial landscape. Corporations will have to redesign themselves if they are to reconcile the need to constantly update the technological infrastructure with a newly demanding investment community.

In the next chapter, we will reveal a new source of wealth to sit alongside physical and intellectual capital – relational capital – and show how that could be the salvation of struggling corporations in both the new and old economies.

CHAPTER 6

Relational Capital

INTRODUCTION

We have mapped out the way that a combination of forces has changed and will continue to change the business environment. Now it is time to look at how corporations should adapt, not just to survive, but to succeed in this new world. We have already alluded to atomization – the idea that smaller units will be the key to an effective response – but now we will explain what it is about that process that unlocks the potential of the corporation.

We should also be able to lay some fears to rest by demonstrating that this seemingly destructive process will, in fact, enhance rather than diminish shareholder value. In that sense we will be splitting the atom to unleash previously confined forces. And the key concept that underpins all this will be relational capital, the unexplored value of existing relationships that can now be extracted because of the ease with which the Web enables us to manage previously rigid networks.

THREE FACTORS INFLUENCING WEALTH CREATION

The formula for shareholder value introduced in the previous chapter helps explain the current de-emphasis on discounted cash flow of current operations, but does not develop any new indicators for corporate success.

Our work, both at Cap Gemini Ernst & Young and as part of a global multi-client program – Business in The Third Millennium – has identified three main factors that contribute to shareholder wealth. The first is a sharp focus on stakeholder relationships, meaning the anticipation and awareness of stakeholder needs (both articulated and latent), in particular those of the customer.

The second is the development of inter-business value networks, formed of the partnerships and alliances that will become the chief means of delivering value to all the stakeholders in the connected economy. They will include suppliers to the business and other trading partners – even traditional competitors.

And last but very importantly, successful organizational forms will need to show high levels of agility and creativity – what we call innovative capacity. These characteristics will be best enabled by a knowledge-intensive structure and a high-trust environment.

Knowledge is best extracted and re-used in an atmosphere of high trust. For example, a customer is willing to share intimate thoughts if a supplier respects his or her trust and responds with offerings that are relevant and thus more beneficial. The future world of intimate relationships emerging from two-way connectivity will only materialize in a high-trust environment. These three factors – stakeholder relationships, value network management, and innovative capacity – provide the basis for a new formula for business competitiveness in the new economy (Fig. 6.1).

RELATIONSHIPS GENERATE INCREASING VALUE

Examine any large organization and you will find a multiplicity of relationships that are sustained over time. The four most obvious are with customers, suppliers, employees and shareholders. Much of the infrastructure of any organization is concerned with building and maintaining these associations through core functions like sales and marketing, procurement, human resources

$$
\text{Shareholder value} = \left(\text{Customer intimacy} + \text{Value networking} \right) \times \text{Innovation capacity}
$$

Fig. 6.1   Shareholder value equation.

BUSINESS IN THE THIRD MILLENNIUM

Following closely in the footsteps of MIT's "Management in the Nineties" program, Business in the Third Millennium was initiated by Gill Ringland, group
director of strategy with ICL Fujitsu, to create a global forum for strategic research
into the broader social and economic effects of the digital economy. Under SRI
Consulting's stewardship (and subsequently that of FirstMatter LLC – the futures
consultancy spin-off of SRI), the program brought together a further nine sponsors from Europe, America and the Far East. These included public and private
organizations such as Barclays Bank, BP Amoco, Chevron, EPRI, the European
Commission, the Gas Research Council, NTT and the US Postal Service.

The research of the program was focused on those forces of high impact,
high uncertainty that were a direct consequence of digital technology. A central
theme of the program was the blurring of relationships between individuals
in society, major corporations and national governments brought about by the
wide spread adoption of the Internet. Early areas of focus included evolution
of digital infrastructures, digital literacy, changing market segmentation, and
new sources of shareholder value. The program had a multiplicity of service
delivery elements, including quarterly meetings of sponsors, regular research
reports and position papers, on-site client briefings and a community Web site.
Of key importance to the research was the annual scenario-planning exercise
that reviewed changes in the world economy influenced by digital technology.

The program took advantage of scenario-planning techniques developed
jointly by SRI and Shell in the seventies. Watts Wacker, the Resident Futurist of
SRI and co-founder of FirstMatter provided much of the thought leadership for
the program. Roger Camrass was the program director from inception in 1992
to completion in 1998.

and investor relations. Each of these stakeholders is probably a customer,
employee, shareholder or supplier of another corporation, and so we have a
web of relationships forming a potential source of value in the new economy
(Fig. 6.2).

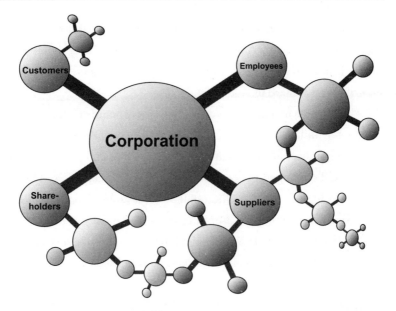

Fig. 6.2 Relationships with key stakeholders.

In addition to these primary examples, large corporations can have as many as 40 or 50 other relationships with key stakeholders like governments, local communities, the media and other interest groups.

Let us look at one of the most valuable relationships – that with the customer. A key business process of any organization is the acquisition and retention of its key customers – those that contribute to business profitability. In the connected economy, many alternative channels, on-land and on-line, are employed to sustain these relationships, ranging from direct sales and tele-marketing to Web-based techniques like Web sites and portals. The cost of customer acquisition can be high both on the ground and in cyberspace, as dot.com corporations have found to their cost. Media- and incentive-spends of up to several hundred dollars per new consumer are commonly built in to business plans for those corporations using the World Wide Web as its primary channel for customer acquisition.

The importance of this customer acquisition process is reflected in the capital value of new Web-based or "on-line" corporations. Amazon.com commands a market valuation that is based on a multiple of the total number of acquired customers – the traditional market valuation based on the use of price to earnings is not meaningful while the corporation continues to be loss making.

These multiples have ranged between $5000 and $20,000 per customer in recent months, valuing Amazon.com in the tens of billions of dollars. A similar metric is used to value cable franchises where each home passed by the cable contributes $3–5000 to total capital value.

In the area of human resources, the cost of acquiring talented employees can be far higher than that associated with customer acquisition. For many service organizations, the total cost of acquisition and profitable deployment of new staff can equal between two and three years of pay and benefits. This may be as high as half-a-million dollars for a professional services organization, where the employees are, in essence, the means of production. Again, this provides a legitimate way of calculating the value of a services corporation based on the multiple of employees and their individual market valuation.

RELATIONSHIPS CONSIST OF COMPLEX INTERACTIONS

Traditional approaches to improving business performance were often based on minimizing the cost of building and supporting key stakeholder relationships. Re-engineering, for example, focused on corporate downsizing, which reduced the number of employees and simplified supplier and customer arrangements. These efforts were aimed at cutting the cost of doing business rather than increasing the economic benefits arising from established relationships.

According to *Blur*, authored by CGEY's Stan Davis and Chris Meyer, any relationship in a connected world represents a complex exchange of financial, emotional and contextual information. In their words, a relationship consists of a six-lane highway where value is created through constant interactions (Fig. 6.3).

In the connected economy, managers are now being tasked with extracting additional value from established relationships through the use of electronic, interactive channels and Web-based electronic markets. One of the oil majors has traffic of over twenty million customers per week through its retail forecourts – that is the good news. However, the interaction with each customer is limited to a basic transaction where minimal information is exchanged. Not surprisingly this same corporation is now planning to install Internet connec-

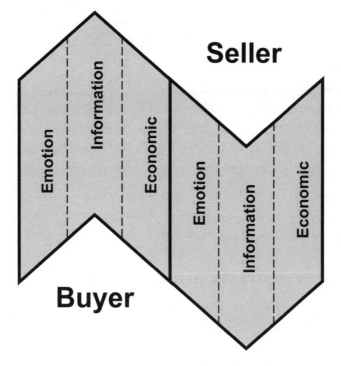

Source: Blur by Stan Davis and Chris Meyer

Fig. 6.3   The six-lane exchange highway.

tions into all its main retail outlets to encourage a far wider level of customer interaction. The potential prize is enormous – consider an Amazon.com multiple of $5000 for each retail customer. This could amount to an additional $100 billion of equity value, worth a 30 percent increase in the share price. This is the fusion of old- and new-economy business practice to improve corporate value.

ELECTRONIC MARKETS CREATE VALUE OUT OF EXISTING RELATIONSHIPS

Other mechanisms for enhancing value have emerged from marketplaces such as Covisint – the electronic market that sits between leading car manufacturers such as GM and Ford, and the many thousands of component suppliers that serve these corporations. These markets exploit Web-based trading and collaboration mechanisms to increase the economic value flowing between suppliers and customer organizations. By so doing, they can create new pockets of shareholder value.

While many of the new marketplaces will fail (see Chapter 8), the prize for the winners is enormous. In the case of Covisint, there has been speculation that shareholder value would be measured in the tens of billions once the company was brought to market. *This is new value that did not exist before the creation of the e-marketplace.* The transactional information gathered within the e-marketplace will also have value within the sector and could spawn secondary markets based on derivatives. These, in turn, will further increase value opportunities like those that exist in financial exchanges.

PORTALS HELP TO EXTEND RELATIONSHIPS

Introducing Web-based techniques to generate new value opportunities is now broadening out from customers to include additional classes of stakeholder such as employees. Shared Internet portals will provide a range of services, financial and other, to employees of several different corporations. Service providers might offer insurance, investment, banking and home shopping. And the spending power of the audience brought together by these worksite marketing opportunities promise tremendous value for their operators, another new source of wealth that will be shared with the portal, the employer and employee. As with any corporate scheme, like healthcare, the e-HR portal can aggregate demand across many thousands of staff to produce mutual benefits of scope and scale. And extending these portals across corporations could lead to career secondment in addition to the usual aggregation opportunities.

Devices like electronic markets and portals are relationship enablers, and we can expect an explosion of activity within traditional organizations focused on identifying and extracting these new sources of value. In this respect, old-economy organizations have a formidable advantage against new-economy corporations who have few if any established relationships to capitalize on. This may be sufficient to boost ailing stock prices in the short term, but how will these corporations increase their share of the overall economic pie?

RELATIONSHIPS ARE ACCELERATED BY TRUST

Trust has long been the core to successful commercial relationships. Long before electronic means of communications, the handshake represented a mutual commitment to a commercial transaction. With the scale and complexity of modern business, the opportunities to develop personal relationships based on trust are less frequent. Instead, corporations develop brand promises to reinforce their commitment to mass communities, be they customers, employees or shareholders. The credibility of a brand is based on the ability of a corporation to repeatedly deliver its promise. In the words of the eminent futurist, Watts Wacker, trust is a promise kept. Relationships of all kinds are built and sustained by trust. In the modern business world, brand is a natural extension to the trust embodied in personal relationships.

Consider one of the most valuable stakeholders in any business – the customer. As explained by Treacy and Wiersema in their book *Disciplines of Market Leadership*, until now successful businesses have delivered their value proposition to customers through one of essentially three models:[1]

- Many successful corporations, like Dell and McDonalds, operate within a model of *operational excellence*, aiming to excel at delivering a product that is cheap to purchase and represents acceptable quality. The customer develops trust in consistency.
- Alternatively, *product leadership* (think Intel and Sony) means adopting a strategy that focuses primarily on continuous innovation and creativity, constantly introducing new products and improving existing ones. The customer is attracted by the sense of unrelenting improvement.
- Finally, *customer intimacy* is a model that stresses customer service and care. The business is organized around close customer relationships and personalization of products and services. The customer feels like an individual in the eyes of the supplier.

The traditional view is that any business must show adequate performance in all three of these sources of customer value, but that it should aim to excel in one only. That remains so. But in a digital economy built on a myriad of electronic connections, a fourth source of value – *managing trust in the brand* – will become critical for all businesses. Unless you actively manage your brand, the added value that you bring will not be recognized by customers.

This is also the case for other stakeholders, who view a corporation mainly through its brand promise. Employees will place their loyalty with a corporation whose brand they respect such as Disney, Nokia or Coca-Cola. In many cases this reflects a statement of lifestyle, or personal aspiration, as in the case of BMW where the brand communicates the "ultimate driving experience."

We expect that as the connected economy expands, the majority of stakeholder interactions will migrate towards electronic channels like Web-based portals. This is becoming commonplace for many customer interactions, and will shortly extend to employees as e-HR portals become viable. Cisco, for one, has already evolved beyond this point, and could well claim to have become an entirely virtual organization where the Web is the single point of contact for internal and external parties. In such circumstances, the power of the corporate promise, as reflected in the brand, is the one lever to accelerate the wide number of relationships needed for success.

BUSINESS NETWORKS: VALUE GENERATED THROUGH CO-OPERATION

The scale and pace of change will make it increasingly difficult for corporations to be vertically integrated and undertake all business functions alone. The recent trend towards outsourcing will also evolve further as we will see in later chapters. Businesses will increasingly join up with others to create co-operative supply relationships. Formal alliances and informal networks with

---

CISCO SYSTEMS

Cisco Systems is a world leader, and perhaps *the* world leader, in the use of virtual technologies and Web-based systems in its everyday business. It realized, earlier than most, that transaction costs could be lower and quality improved by using the Internet to shape every encounter with its customers, employees, partners and suppliers. At the heart of Cisco is an intricate Internet-based network

---

linking all aspects of its value web, and which it claims provides annual savings of over $800m. This is in addition to a range of other upside benefits such as increased customer satisfaction, reduced product development times, inventory reduction and increases in productivity.

Cisco rebuilt itself around three private webs, which drive Web-based systems and processes into the core of every commercial activity. Firstly, Cisco Connection Online (CCO) deals with customer-facing processes, using the Internet as a collaborative platform to improve customer service around the world. CCO is accessed approximately 1.5m times each month. More than 80 percent of Cisco's technical support for customers and resellers is delivered in this way, saving it $200m annually. In some ways, this mirrors the Customer Manager atoms that we will discuss in the next chapter.

Secondly, through Cisco Manufacturing Connection Online (MCO), Cisco has created an extranet application in the manufacturing, supply and logistics functions among its globally networked partners. MCO makes available real-time manufacturing information for all the members of its supply web, internal and external, allowing it to run a network of manufacturing atoms. Information made available in this way includes forecast data, inventory and purchase orders, as well as all necessary approvals and alerts from a host of individual manufacturing systems.

Thirdly, the Cisco Employee Connection (CEC) deals with all internal employee self-service initiatives, providing the basis of Service Platform atom(s). CEC allows Cisco to scale its workforce and absorb other companies rapidly without incurring unnecessary overheads. CEC covers the whole spectrum of interval activities with applications to deal with engineering, sales, marketing, training, finances, HR, facilities and procurement.

One of the main reasons Cisco is able to maintain such a complex Internet-based network is its strict enforcement of a simple technology-standards policy. The Cisco model may be attractive and they may make it look easy, but it does not come cheap. Early on in the transformation process Cisco spent in excess of $100m on a complete overhaul of its internal systems and the laying of a robust end-to-end network.

peers, rivals, and even industry participants in traditionally unrelated sectors, will be created to exploit new opportunities to deliver value to customers. And these value networks will help to respond quickly to changing business conditions and increase the competitiveness of network partners. In Korea, the success of Daewoo (a large conglomerate in automobiles and heavy machinery) can be attributed largely to the corporation's effectiveness in forming alliances and partnerships outside Korea. That this wasn't enough to prevent its subsequent downfall is probably due to the giant's inability to update its internal structure.

This trend towards co-operative networks means a change in focus. The focus of many businesses during the 1980s and early 1990s was around the improvement of internal processes though process redesign and re-engineering. More recently, processes have been reoriented to include customers and suppliers, spanning the entire supply chain. For example, in the automotive sector, OEMs (original equipment manufacturers) have integrated their information systems with those of their suppliers. Ford's Valencia and Portuguese manufacturing plants are typical examples where suppliers are located on the same sites as Ford in order to facilitate just-in-time manufacture and close co-operation between the suppliers and Ford.

Over the next decade, this practice will be extended to include peers, and even traditional rivals. Value networks will be formed between businesses in very different industries. For example, in the UK a retailer (Sainsbury), a bank (Bank of Scotland), and a telecom service provider (BT) are co-operating in providing a home shopping service.

Trusting relationships will become an essential ingredient of successful value networks. These informal relationships should not be regarded as a substitute for proper contractual arrangements. Indeed, the development of contractual arrangements can be used to build trust. But however carefully contracts are constructed, they can rarely foresee all possible outcomes in the relationship between parties. For example, MG Rover, the UK car manufacturer, embarked on a partnership contract for the provision of its network services. When there was a major failure in the network, the provider agreed to pay MG Rover compensation voluntarily. There was no provision in the contract between the parties for compensation, but the voluntary payment ensured that the parties could continue to trust each other, even if on occasions things do go wrong.

With an increasing emphasis on value networks, relationship management, and trust, the competitive perspective is shifting. Competition in the future may be less between individual firms and more between the value networks in which they participate – perhaps between temporary virtual *keiretsu*. Increasingly the participants in the network will also co-ordinate, co-operate, and co-create new opportunities. Glass and ceramics manufacturer Corning Glass, for example, has always maintained a brisk rate of product and technology innovation by creating marketing alliances with other corporations to penetrate new markets. It does what it knows best, but it will not encroach on the marketing competencies of its partners in order to help facilitate collective growth.

ORGANIZATIONAL AGILITY AND CREATIVITY

The third factor in our new equation for shareholder value is innovative capacity – related to its internal agility and creativity. This implies speed and originality of thought and action. An innovative organization is one that quickly recognizes significant changes in the external environment and imaginatively reconfigures its resources to exploit them. It may well use the intelligence derived from the value networks that surround it as its primary stimulus, but the core of its success will be the knowledge and creativity that reside within. We describe such entities as "smart companies" in our atomized world. How do smart companies gain advantage?

With the advent of the World Wide Web, two particular advantages arise. The first is the expanded access to a wide spectrum of intellectual property through Web-based search engines. There are several such search engines in operation today like PATEX.com and Yet2Come.com. Many thousands of organizations contribute their intellectual property in the form of patents and inventions to these sites, in return for possible new research opportunities and IP transactions.

The second advantage emerges from the possibilities of broader co-operation with experts inside and outside the organization. Web-based collaborative tools enable complex interactions to be conducted between remote experts. These tools remove many of the barriers to remote working and foster a sense of community amongst researchers and designers. Human expertise remains the core component of any smart company. But it can be scaled and directed more effectively through intensive use of Web techniques.

Both techniques require a vital enabling component – sophisticated knowledge management – the latter being a product of the Web-enabled environment. Innovation is a soft process that depends on complex human interactions. Knowledge is the common thread that binds these interactions together and increases their value. Many organizations today employ first-generation knowledge management systems, and are keen to progress further. The most important attribute of effective knowledge management however is a cultural one, which is the commitment that individuals have to share their own knowledge within a common community. Again, the desire to do so is based entirely on trust and reciprocity, encouraged by a culture where transferring knowledge, rather than controlling it, is the basis of power.

The most successful "smart companies" will employ a variety of on-line tools for internal and external working. The value of such tools will be further accelerated by a common belief and atmosphere of trust.

TRUST ACCELERATES VALUE

We have argued that shareholder value is a combination of relational capital, value network competence and innovative capacity. Each of these factors is important on its own, but taken as a whole, they indicate how organizations should prepare themselves for the new economy. The common thread between all three factors is the trust that the organization is able to generate, both within itself and to external parties. We thus believe that trust is a common accelerator that has persuaded us to modify the shareholder equation accordingly (Fig. 6.4).

Shareholder Value is equal to the sum of Customer Intimacy and Value Networking, multiplied by Innovation Capacity, and accelerated by the power of Trust.

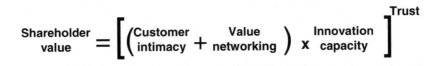

Fig. 6.4 Modified shareholder value equation.

In our view, trust is a hard issue within the connected economy. Most businesses know that competitive survival depends on such factors as effective cash management, stock control and distribution efficiency, product and process innovation, and product quality – what one might call " hard" management issues. They are, and will continue to be, important.

But alone they will not be enough to differentiate one business from another in a future global world where products, processes, and markets become increasingly similar. Trust in the brand, trust between business partners, and internal trust will become essential in building healthy ecological competitive business relationships.

Some managers may feel uncomfortable with what they regard as a soft issue. But trust is an asset of the business like any other. It should therefore be treated as a hard management issue – perhaps the hardest of all. The ability of a business to create and maintain trust will determine its unique identity as a business, and that is where the source of future competitiveness will lie.

SUMMARY

Corporations are already involved in a complex network of relationships but the Web enables the extraction of previously unexploited value from them all. Electronic channels mean that the relationships can at last be managed effectively to produce something genuinely co-operative. The effect is titanic. It makes it easier than ever for corporations to concentrate on their strengths, while reinforcing relationships by feeding secondary functions to more skilled practitioners elsewhere in the network.

As if this was not a dramatic enough change in corporate behavior in itself, it will trigger another reorientation in the way the business operates. It will shift the competitive focus away from old-style corporate eyeballing, where companies squared up to one another in the consumer arena, towards a world in which the real contest is fought between the networks themselves.

But for all this to happen effectively it will need a reawakening to the virtues of an antique business emotion. Trust. (It's not all gleamingly new. Some things never change.) Trust will be the key differentiation in the context of an increasingly commoditized business environment. It affects every stakeholder relationship and will have to be treated with unprecedented seriousness. Trust will become a "hard" management issue.

PART IV
Destination

By now, it should be pretty clear that we cannot go on as we are. Consumers have grown with the connected economy and our large corporations, with their internal focus, have lost what grasp of reality they ever had. Shares in Monolith, Inc. are not performing and its CEO has to find a way of returning value to the market. Fortunately, the new connectivity lets us take a fresh look at corporate structures.

It is time to unleash the atoms. We will tell you where they come from, how they can be released, and how they will work together. We will look at how to create a business case for atomization, and take a look at atomized versions of today's leading industries.

CHAPTER 7

Let's Meet the Atoms

A QUICK SUMMARY OF WHERE WE'VE BEEN SO FAR

WELCOME TO THE FOURTH SECTION of the book, in which we lay out our view of the future shape of the economy. For those that skipped over the Departures section, here is a summary of the stuff you missed.

By now it's pretty clear that universal connectivity is rapidly changing our roles as individuals, either as individual employees or individual customers, from one of response to one of demand. We in the developed world finally have a way of expressing all of our demands, and those demands are to *increase our experience* rather than to *consume your product*.

It's also clear that most corporations are not ready to respond to this change in role, being too centered on their products and their internal functions. A new focus on agility is needed, and as you can't be big and agile at the same time (the internal cost of movement is too high), fragmentation is looking more and more attractive. For many of the players in the economy, "critical mass" now translates as "critically ill."

Meanwhile, the market capitalization of the traditional giants continues to drop, and the corporations that are winning the battle for shareholder trust (the only real safeguard of CEO survival) are agile and relationship-focused. If the giants are to survive in any form, their CEOs must find a way to unlock the relational capital tied up in their organization.

At the same time, the equilibrium between internal and external transaction costs has shifted. Sure, internal Web enablement will streamline process, but the costs of doing business with other organizations will drop further and faster. This challenges the old logic about corporate size at the most inconvenient time possible.

Individual demands are pushing an unstable system and the only possible outcome is radical change. For those who embrace it, the prize in terms of unlocked relational capital is enormous. The change will take time – we think it will be another ten years before its new shape becomes clear but that doesn't mean we won't see it happening. The next decade will feel like snowboarding in front of an avalanche.

And as for the rest of the book, we are going to look at the communications channels that will link the new players to one another and to their customers, explore the hidden sources of relational capital in your organization, and learn to identify the atoms. Then we will discuss how to make these atoms successful and how to manage them, predict some industry-wide changes, and then offer a brief guide to starting the process rolling.

But first, this chapter.

INTRODUCTION

This is where we take a big step forward. We have dismantled everything that makes up your familiar business environment and now we need to describe how it gets put back together. And this involves introducing you to a new set of reconstituted sub-components – our atoms. Bear with us while we familiarize you with what will initially be alien concepts. We think you will quickly see how they prepare corporations for the future in a way that leaves existing structures gasping for air.

Remember – the demands of the future will be flexibility, agility, an unprecedented outward-looking interface, and a sensitivity to the fact that effective relationship management is critical if you are to succeed. A failure to embed the concept of relational value into core business practice will undermine any hope of keeping pace with the rest of the network. And where there is more at stake than just your own success and survival you can expect rough treatment from your collaborators.

LET'S MEET THE ATOMS

Looking the wrong way

With a roll of drums and a short fanfare, it's time to take a look at the business models that we think will emerge to support the new economy.

Most large corporations today are good at producing things. They excel at operational efficiency, asset management etc., and focus on getting the best out of their means of production. Even allegedly customer-centric organizations like retail banks are organized into branches, offices, processing centers etc., that reflect the organization's needs for productivity more than they do the convenience of the customers.

But most organizations also try to be conduits of demand, without ever approaching the levels of customer intimacy that this requires. It's not just a knowledge of your customer's name and credit card number, but a real understanding of what motivates them. It also requires an organization structure that accepts that you exist to serve the customer rather than the customer existing to consume your products. Instead we see huge proportions of the cost of the corporation's products being spent on marketing and sales in an attempt to maintain an artificial level of demand.

So we can say that today's corporations attempt to combine demand capture with production competency, and usually fail miserably. This is the worst of all possible worlds – trying to understand the customer while being structurally unable to do so. But there is hope – if we unbundle those dimensions of focus and competence, we find our first three atoms (Fig. 7.1).

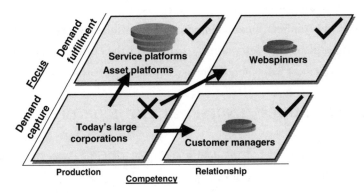

Fig. 7.1 Decoupling competency and focus.

Keep it simple

Competency in production is a fine thing to have if you are prepared to concentrate on efficient and profitable operations and accept that others will be better at understanding consumers. We foresee two types of production-focused business platforms emerging, and we shall call those based around capital-intensive services *asset platforms* to distinguish them from atom types based around manpower-intensive services, or *service platforms*. Both types will make their money from superb efficiency, freed from the distractions of consumer management.

If, on the other hand, you genuinely do have a deep and intimate knowledge of individuals and are able to turn their emotions into demands, then this is a hugely valuable source of relational capital – why not become a *customer manager* and let others concentrate on fulfilling that demand? After all, now that external transaction costs are falling, you can source the things the customer needs more effectively and cheaply.

The combination of relationship competency without direct, high-quality, access to the consumer is also a good place to be. With the shape of the economy changing around you, an ability to forge alliances that connect together elements of an offer is again an unexploited source of relationship capital. We will call these creators of the value web *webspinners*.

A fourth type of entity, concentrating on knowledge as an asset and trading on intellectual excellence and innovation, spans all of these categories. We will come to these *smart companies* in the next section. We will also introduce the *portfolio owner*, which owns the rest of the atoms.

So these are our basic atoms – two types of business platforms, customer managers, webspinners, smart companies and portfolio owners. Some of these atoms will be genuinely new entities, particularly the customer managers, but it is likely that most will emerge from within the large corporations.

SMART COMPANIES – ENGINES OF THE ECONOMY

A smart company is an independent knowledge-based business, capitalizing on its skills in innovation. It may concentrate on science and technology (e.g. drug research, specialist software, equipment design), or in more creative fields (graphic design, advertising, journalism). In some ways, these are the engines of human endeavor, the ways by which the economy moves itself forward.

Many of these smart companies will be formed from consultancies, consulting engineers, designers, architects etc., and others will be carved out of existing corporations: innovation is an art that is too often crushed by size, although you sometimes find it in semi-autonomous specialist elements concentrating on process or product improvement.

But why should a corporation share its intellectual assets? Because if one of these semi-autonomous elements knows how to build a better mousetrap, or has a better mousetrap-construction process, then this item of intellectual property has an asset value in its own right. If it has enough ideas, the chances are that the market can find more to do with the ideas in its portfolio than can one corporation. The portfolio can therefore be securitized and bring capital wealth or income to its parent corporation.

It is wrong to look at the value of these smart corporations, which will always be relatively small, in the same light as large corporations. Their value is determined by the worth of their patents, their innovation and knowledge-reuse processes, and the relationships they can exploit to realize value from the ideas. As with many R&D operations – where for every successful drug there are 10, 100 or 1000 unsuccessful ones – their profits may depend on only one or two positive outcomes. Intangible worth will make up the principal element of the share price, with a solid long-term growth in capital worth to more than compensate for the lack of profits (although in the short term the ride will often be very exciting).

WEBSPINNERS – BUSINESS CATALYSTS

As we saw in Chapter 2, high external transaction costs have always meant that business-to-business relationships in the old production-centered world tended to be governed by pre-ordained agreements – "we might buy so much of this kind of stuff from you, at this price." But in a world where the customers' wishes can be tapped and must be followed, these rigid chains will be too inflexible. When no two offers are likely to be identical, the elements of the offer that are to be assembled – and therefore the business-to-business bonds that need to be created – vary almost in real time.

Using third parties to find out who offers, or wants to buy, goods or services is almost as old as commerce itself. The rise of rich, ubiquitous and (most importantly) two-way communications channels promises to make it much easier to establish who you could partner with, up to and including creating alliances at the moment of trade. In a world where large, vertically-integrated corporations and their supply chains start to fragment many more business relationships will be needed and there will be many more potential offers to evaluate.

While the new e-commerce technologies reduce the sourcing and management elements of transaction costs, there is currently little that can be done about discovery costs – finding out *who* you should be dealing with, for other than simple commodities – and that is the role of the webspinner atoms. They will own the relationships between suppliers and customers across the value chain by improving the matching process. To continue with our chemistry analogy, they act as catalysts to ease the bond-making and bond-breaking processes.

Deciding to trade with someone is a complex mixture of price, trust and prior experience. It's not just a question of who can provide the goods or services you need, but whether or not the goods or services are available now, and whether the potential partner can be trusted to deliver. The webspinner will facilitate inventory visibility and complete description of the goods or services, and must provide an assurance of trustworthiness.

That assurance of trustworthiness is the key to the webspinner's value proposition. Generated from a combination of financial status, transaction history and rigorous review by previous trading partners, webspinners could offer anything from basic "trust ratings" to full guarantee of supply and payment.

Webspinners are also the natural gateways for other service providers that facilitate trade (such as insurance, procurement advice, protection against currency fluctuation and bankruptcy, import/export services, shipping, and advice on legal and cultural differences). It is the arrangement of these services that will generate most of their revenue rather than simple transaction or introduction fees.

ENRON – CHANGING ATOM TYPES

Enron used to be an energy provider, albeit with a broadband communications arm. It still operates power stations but it's now in the coal, gas, electricity, water, finance, insurance, emissions trading and derivatives businesses and shows no signs of stopping there. In a period of a year the company doubled its market capitalization while the rest of the industry remained stagnant. How did it pull that one off?

The first step in the journey was identification and concentration on the core, just as we describe in Chapter 10. In mid-1999 it sold off its core oil and gas subsidiary to concentrate on "distribution, wholesale and energy-related services."

In October 1999 Enron launched its first Internet marketplace, EnronOnline, trading energy derivatives and emissions credits. While there are many such marketplaces nowadays, this was revolutionary in its time. Its purpose is to connect buyers and sellers together to trade specialist items, sometimes with Enron making the market.

For example, if you are building a new power station, you may not be using your current emissions credits although you may not have enough in ten years time. EnronOnline will connect you with someone with the opposite profile to arrange an emissions swap, or perhaps to trade the credits for some electricity.

In addition, EnronOnline now trades specialist shipping, credit risk, pipeline capacity, metals, chemicals and a host of other products. By the end of 2000, EnronOnline was handling $3bn of transactions. Something like 60 percent of Enron's own transactions go through this marketplace.

It has also spawned a number of specialist marketplaces. For example, in 1998, a heatwave in the US Midwest increased the short-term price of electricity 500-fold. Enron's response was to set up a derivatives marketplace (with the marvelous slogan "Buy the weather you want"), where distributors, farmers and companies can buy weather-related options to minimize their risk (www.weatherdesk.com). Similarly, they set up another enterprise called Enron-Credit which facilitates trade by allowing corporations to buy what is effectively insurance against their trading partners going bankrupt, and water2water.com is a derivatives market for the water industry. And sometimes Enron makes the market itself – clickpaper.com allows its customers to buy and sell pulp, paper and wood products (with Enron guaranteeing the transaction and taking a spread on the products).

What Enron has done here is spawn a host of webspinners, connecting parties together for the good of the industry, even in industries in which it was not particularly active. But Enron is also active in sales of products to customers, both in Europe and the US. In the US, it formed a partnership (see www.newpowercompany.com) between Enron's asset platform for power generation, a horizontal IT service platform (IBM) to operate the service and an emerging customer manager (AOL) to market it.

Reality check ... this is an *energy* company! It just doesn't think like an energy company.

Did it work? Between the end of October 1999, when the first marketplace was announced, and the end of October 2000, Enron had doubled its share price, while the rest of the oil industry had shown about five percent growth. This is not dot.com froth – the increased market capitalization survived the collapse of NASDAQ in 2000. By Enron's figures[1] its wholesale services division was worth $50bn in January 2001, making up 45 percent of Enron's total valuation.

So by creating new multi-billion-dollar webspinner atoms, and by forming alliances with other atom types to get its products to market, Enron was able to unlock sufficient relational capital to *double* its share price in a year.

CUSTOMER MANAGERS – KNOWING THE INDIVIDUAL

Yahoo!'s stated vision has hardly changed since 1994: "...the only place anyone has to go to find something, connect to someone or buy anything."[2] Wow! If they were *the* only place that we needed to go on the Internet, where all of our news (whether from our various communities of interest or from the wider world), our shopping, our finances etc. came from, think of the capital value of those relationships! That's a grand vision, equivalent to most of the business done by one billion people going through a single branch of Wal-Mart.

But Yahoo!'s vision is perhaps too large. It's more likely that the capture of customer desires and delivery of satisfaction will be focused around some of the customer's macro-processes – learning, health, personal wealth management, employability,[3] entertainment etc. – with bundles created, not to meet the typical customer's need, but your particular preferences.

This idea of *your* preference is key. Anyone who has used Amazon.com frequently will know that they encourage you to review the goods you have bought from them so that they can provide better recommendations on what you might like in future – providing insider knowledge of your likes and dislikes in return for better service. The customer portal must capture, confirm, re-confirm and constantly use the customer's views and experiences (and those of other, seemingly similar customers) in suggesting offers.

This presents some practical difficulties – in some European countries it is illegal to mine customer data in this way. But if you can persuade the customers to give you information about themselves (and that persuasion might be expensive) and if you use the information they share with you to improve their lives, then their loyalty and a major share of their wallet is assured for ever.[4] That's why we expect the best customer managers will have revenues measured in tens of millions of dollars per employee and solid growth in capital worth.

Who will form these most valuable of corporations? We'll talk more about that in subsequent chapters, but it is far from certain that it will be today's large corporations. Many organizations with large retail chains (including oil corporations and banks) know little about their customers and have even less idea what to do with the knowledge. Talking about assuming management of the customers' lifestyle is fanciful for the moment. The key idea that most large corporations are struggling with is that it's what customer intimacy can do for the customer that matters, not what it can do for them.

One exception is the UK supermarket chain, Tesco, and we profile them in the case study below.

TESCO – BECOMING A CUSTOMER MANAGER

Although now the UK's leading grocery retailer, Tesco has traditionally been at the lower end of the market. It pulled out of this position by learning about its customers and being prepared to use that knowledge, and through excellence in Web-based customer service.

The story starts a decade ago, when the company started to build a customer database around its loyalty card scheme. If you (loyally) present your card at the checkout you receive a one percent discount on your purchases. 15 million customers (about a third of the adult population) belong to this loyalty scheme, including one of our colleagues in the UK. Like most other UK supermarkets, Tesco has an "affiliate marketing" deal with a number of non-competing organizations to provide financial services etc.[5] During the later stages of his wife's pregnancy, our colleague used the supermarket's Web site to buy his son's first disposable diapers, and shortly afterwards he received a mailshot from the supermarket's banking affiliate about planning for school fees! This could be a coincidence, but in a time when some retailers see their loyalty card schemes bringing little benefit, we see this as an example of a corporation who can not only deduce information about its customers but who can identify major lifestyle events from the individual's purchasing patterns. Now that's customer intimacy.

But it's Tesco's Web presence that particularly excites us. Tesco is the world's largest Internet grocer, keeping 300 of its stores open overnight to fulfill orders. Items ordered on-line are delivered the next day for a £5 ($7) delivery charge. The service is popular with time-harried users that still make up the majority of the UK surfing population, and its customers get good prices, discounts and (above all) increased convenience. The loyalty card scheme is used throughout to reward repeat buying and personalize the site. And Tesco, of course, increases its understanding of the customer with each purchase.

The core grocery products are supplemented by non-competing products and services, and the range far exceeds that carried by Tesco's physical stores. Some products (books, CDs, furniture, jewellery, gifts, ISP) are delivered from other providers but with the Tesco brand, while others are co-branded (financial services from Royal Bank of Scotland, and flowers from Interflora). This affiliate marketing means increased revenues for Tesco and decreased cost for all participants, with the best-known brand being used to promote the goods.

Finally, Tesco's brand and image is enhanced, and its product set moved from "groceries" into "lifestyle," a move supported by Tesco's purchase of a large stake in the UK version of iVillage, a women's lifestyle portal. We see Tesco as being one of the few companies likely to make the transformation from retailer into customer manager.

ASSET-BASED BUSINESS PLATFORMS – SCALE HAS ITS PLACE

The types of atoms we have described up to now are fine but they can only marshal and reorganize – they aren't actually creating the physical goods that are probably going to be an element of the customer offer. *Someone* has to make the cars, grow the bananas and refine the oil, and that's where we reach the fourth type of Atomic Corporation, the asset-based business platforms (we will call them *asset platforms* for short).

What are the characteristics of this type of organization? Most of them are concerned with the manipulation and movement of matter on a grand scale within a particular industry, and here critical mass can play a part. We foresee these platforms being multinational and potentially global, either through direct ownership or by a franchising arrangement.

Businesses in this category will require considerable capital and be focused on operational excellence within a single industry, looking for economies of scale and scope in the manufacturing and distribution of products and services. They will be the largest players in our atomized economy in terms of numbers of people, capital employed and (probably) revenues and profit. But they won't dominate the supply chain – they are too far from the customer for that to happen.

We can see from today's stock market that large-scale capital businesses tend to have stable (and low) market capitalizations, but produce solid profits. Looking at corporations like Ford, General Motors, airlines, agribusinesses etc., we can see corporations with price/earnings ratios often of less than ten, but which give good dividend yields. These atoms will be the blue chip investments of tomorrow, offering good returns at relatively low risk.

That isn't to say that there is no scope for the small, specialist refinery, the specialist farmer, the microbrewery, or the corner shop. They will trade efficiency for agility and play their role in providing customized services, albeit at higher cost than the global giants.

So where will these corporations come from? We are betting that they will (e)merge from parts of today's large corporations and we will discuss how in Chapter 9.

SERVICE PLATFORMS – SPECIALIZING IN THE GENERIC

All of these atoms will need to pay their staff, use office space and computers, file their annual accounts, handle cash and do the thousands of things which do not differentiate them or directly provide income, but which need to be done in order to stay in business. We definitely see a role for a fifth atom type to handle these processes – if you like, to specialize in the generic.

Unlike the vertically-focused asset-based platforms, these generic processes and supporting platforms would not be specific to one industry, but would probably be tied to a geography or to a legal system. An atom which provides HR support processes in the US, for example, would not be viable in the European Union because of the differences between labor laws, tax structures and retirement planning mechanisms.

Here are some examples of how horizontal service platforms might be created and how they could work:

- *Procurement* – the first Internet marketplaces to emerge were horizontal marketplaces set up by banks and telcos. These marketplaces managed catalogues and the purchasing element of the process, and many of them (especially those created by banks) had ambitions to support the payment and reconciliation process. It is a short step to envisage the full life-cycle of procurement being managed by a horizontal platform, especially for indirect items, with aggregated spend being put to good use by specialist negotiators. In the next chapter, we profile one such marketplace, CoNext.

■ *Office space* – this ties up a great deal of capital but adds little value. It is hard to find, troublesome to maintain and difficult to get rid of. A specialist supplier with a large pool of quality office space could lease it and dispose of it quickly. Again, we profile one such supplier, Regus, below.

■ *Human relations* – while most corporations would describe their employees as their most important asset, very few have a set of HR processes that would seem to reflect that view. All too often, HR processes and systems increase bureaucracy for the worker and block information that could allow them to do their job better. The door is open for entities with superb support infrastructures to sweep away most of the poor quality in-house organizations and serve many corporations within the same geography.

Other potential areas for horizontal service platforms would be:

■ marketing, publicity, lobbying, and events management;
■ management of customer response units (e.g. call centers) and customer insight processes (surveys, market research, demographics etc.);
■ IT (development, operations, maintenance); and
■ business finance (loans, credit management, factoring, insurance, audit, IPOs) and specialist international finance (Forex markets, trade facilitation, letters of credit).

REGUS – "WALK IN, SIT DOWN, START WORK."

It's expensive to maintain branch offices in many locations. CEO Mark Dixon founded the company in 1989 with operations in a single business center in Brussels, selected to help international companies gain instant access to the European marketplace. Twelve years later he had built Regus into the world's largest operator of outsourced business centers, 80 percent of whose business is made up from global corporations like GlaxoSmithKline and Merrill Lynch.

The process for acquiring an international office for a day is fast (they based the rental agreement on a car hire form) and Regus offer business centers in 48 countries where you can rent offices fully equipped with furniture, IT systems, and support staff.

It makes little business sense to maintain under-utilized office space in multiple locations just in case an employee or two need to use it every now and again. One of the main drivers of the success of Regus is the fundamental shift in the relationship between workers and the workplace. Technological advances mean that workers are no longer tied to a single location but can (and do) move to wherever they are most needed.

The rate of change in corporation size has also accelerated, with businesses expanding and contracting with alarming speed. The best corporate planning departments in the world are unable to meet in-house the demands for office space that are demanded by these accelerated life cycles. But perhaps the most compelling reason for Regus' success is their ability to get the costly, capital-intensive, premises off the balance sheet of the large corporations.

With their scale and expertise, Regus probably manage offices better than most corporations anyway; they certainly claim to be able to do it cheaper on a fully loaded, per-user basis. If you do want to own the assets, they also provide an outsourced property management service, removing the need to maintain the skills internally.

However, Regus see themselves primarily as service providers and not as property managers (70 percent of its employees are customer-facing).

In many ways Regus are the archetypal horizontal service platform, operating on top of asset-based businesses (they lease most of their property), providing ways of overcoming geographical and temporal constraints to other corporations. Regus has announced that it intends to form alliances with other horizontal providers to support services such as bookkeeping.

This isn't outsourcing

The idea of splitting off generic elements from the corporation, whether those elements be processes or virtual infrastructure (e.g. IT), has been with us for decades. It's called outsourcing, and we two authors work for corporations that excel at it.

But it's important to understand that the creation and use of service platforms is *not* the same as traditional outsourcing. Most outsourcing deals are struck as a way of reducing the support costs of corporations and (sometimes) to get employees off their books. The deals assume a relatively static business environment, with money being made out of superb operation of the status quo and from a premium on changes.

In that sense, outsourcing aims to provide excellence in operational efficiency, and there are plenty of clients who will attest to its success (although there are a few who will not). But what corporations need most to survive in the new economic environment is *flexibility* and *agility* rather than efficient operation of the status quo. For that reason, we think that the traditional types of long-term outsourcing deal are unlikely to survive.

What will replace them? Probably an arrangement where the external service is paid not by the smooth operation of the status quo but by the overall increase in worth (profit or capital) of the client. This will lead to a much more proactive arrangement, and much better negotiated contracts!

PORTFOLIO OWNERS – OWNING THE ZOO

We have painted a picture where our monolithic corporation can be split into a number of potential atoms. But why will the CEO and the shareholders want to do something like that? The corporation's shareholders will rightly expect to be compensated for the loss of direct control over its assets, and they will be: separation of these atoms from their parent corporation will release considerable relational capital (as you'll see further in Chapter 10).

So our final type of atom is a portfolio owner that exists as a way of retaining the residual ownership of other atoms on behalf of the erstwhile shareholders.

Portfolio owners will manage their atoms as a set of investments that are expected to produce returns, maintaining a mix of types of atoms that produces the right profile of risk and reward.

That is similar to the task of the board of directors in today's conglomerate, and that is where we think most of the portfolio owners will come from, although we would also expect today's venture capitalists, and pension/mutual funds to acquire or part-own atoms.

These are the financial giants of the new economy. Portfolio owner atoms will have large market capitalizations and their balanced portfolios will attract much of the direct investment by individuals. They will be the channels by which many of the atoms – too small to float directly on the stock market – will raise capital.

SUMMARY

If we continue with our chemical analogy, we can see the giant corporations dissolving into a soup of much smaller atoms, supplemented by some new entrants, as shown in Fig. 7.2. These atoms will form and re-form business relationships, with specialist atoms creating molecules to fulfill individual customer needs – we discuss how in the next chapter.

But for now you should now be equipped to understand the language of our new atoms, the constituent parts of the connected economy. They are relevant to the whole range of business processes and can be put together in limitless ways. From the customer manager's understanding of the consumer's desires, the webspinner's skill at unlocking the full creative potential of the network, the smart company's innovation, the asset platform's efficient production of tailored goods, through to the financing role of the portfolio owner and the holistic servicing skills of the horizontal service platform, the atoms represent awesome adaptability. Every function is performed by a specialist. Nothing is compromised.

You'll notice how the atoms cluster around what we consider to be the three dimensions of corporate capability in the connected economy– organizational excellence (asset and service platforms), product innovation (smart companies), and customer intimacy (customer managers).

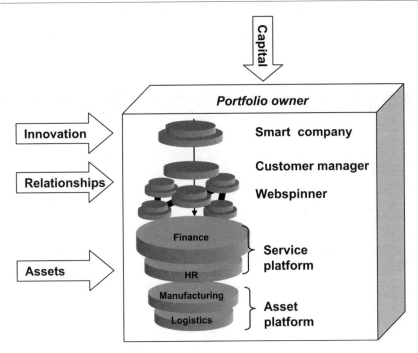

Fig. 7.2 The corporation as a box of atoms.

We predict that by the end of this decade we will be living in a society of Atomic Corporations. Those few behemoths that have yet to make the change will still be running at industrial age speeds. You'll find them clinging to their marketing departments as if they were life vests and watching tearfully as their margins wither away.

There is an evolutionary precedent for this type of change. The dinosaur's ascendancy on earth didn't end overnight, even if it was triggered the moment an asteroid crashed into the Gulf of Mexico. It was ended by the resulting long-term change in the environment that meant it was no longer possible to find the tons of food that were needed to sustain their giant physiques. Smaller, smarter, faster creatures were better at exploiting the changed landscape. And just as the dinosaurs were wiped completely from the face of the earth, so with time, the age of the corporate dinosaur will come to a brutal end.

CHAPTER 8

Making the Molecules Work

INTRODUCTION

IN THE LAST CHAPTER, we introduced the atoms that we think will take over from the giant corporation as the basic units of production and distribution, organizing and re-organizing as needed to meet individual customer demand.

But the structure of an economy is determined through transactions, not organizations, and so we need to look at how the atoms will interact with one another. We need to establish what makes the atoms stick together to form the new molecules of the business world. And that means looking at electronic marketplaces, because we think these will be the bonds of the future. So we will start with a brief introduction to the different types of electronic marketplaces; how they have evolved and will continue to evolve. Then we will take a look at their role in the atomic future. Finally, we will look at exactly how the atoms will link together to form molecules, and consider the implications of globalization, taxation and the regulation of atomic economies.

It is an important lesson of the past few years that excitement predicated on misplaced conceptions of the future can be extremely costly. That's why we think a careful assessment of the direction in which the business environment is headed is critical before you start to contemplate atomization.

MARKETPLACES 101

What are electronic marketplaces? Like their real-world equivalents, they are places where buyers and sellers congregate with the intention of finding someone to trade with. This makes them an important mechanism by which external transaction costs are reduced. Successful marketplaces are defined by strong liquidity,[1] which is partly determined by the size of the population that the market serves. The Internet, with its billion-strong community, was always certain to transform marketplaces and it now looks as if the marketplaces will be an important enabler of the atomization process.

Marketplaces are generally divided into *vertical*, which serve a particular industry, and *horizontal*, which specialize in a particular type of trade across industry boundaries.

Many marketplaces trade only in indirect goods. These are items that corporations consume to keep going, but which do not form part of their end products. Office supplies, tools, travel, temporary labor, spare parts, computers, vehicles and information services all fall into this category. Compared to the superb mechanisms corporations use to make sure of their flow of raw materials, the processes they use for procuring indirect goods are generally awful. So it was no surprise that throughout the late 1990s, most large corporations were implementing or looking at expensive e-procurement systems to automate the purchase of their indirect goods.[2]

Smaller corporations that could not afford their own e-procurement systems saw benefits in using horizontal procurement marketplaces set up by other organizations. These systems allowed the customers to take advantage of pre-negotiated contracts and lower transaction costs, and were normally set up by banks and telcos with the intention of exploiting their base of small customers.

COCA-COLA – A SMART COMPANY

Let's review the principles of atomization by looking at one of the earliest successes – Coca-Cola.

MOLECULAR SODA

The Coca-Cola Corporation is one of the most successful companies in the world. Its brand is a household name in every country in the world. Its P/E ratio is way above that of any other company in its sector and it is one of the most highly-valued businesses of any kind.

How can this be? Despite Coke's revenues being only $20bn per annum, sales of Coca-Cola products amount to over $200bn each year. The Coca-Cola Corporation presides over and supports an enormous and complex molecular web of inter-related businesses who work to make this $200bn figure happen.

All of Coke's manufacturing, bottling, sales and delivery processes are handled by third parties who are controlled through an ingenious cross-shareholding system. So despite the fact that the Coca-Cola Corporation itself actually has minimal involvement in the product, a large part of its value is driven by the power it wields over the global system of third parties who exist to make and handle the product it appears to own.

It closely guards the product formulation secret, it closely guards the use of the Coke brand, and it closely manages the activities of the companies whose job it is to make and deliver the product. But it does not make or sell the end product.

As well as being a portfolio owner, Coke behaves like a smart company. It chose to outsource to this web of businesses all the lower margin manufacturing and distribution elements of its operations in order to focus on being really good at a small number of highly profitable things. Those things are brand management, product formulation and relationship management.

Compare this range of activities with that of PepsiC o. While Coke sought to narrow the scope of activities it was involved in, Pepsi sought to open them up. Coke decided that it was in the beverages industry and that it would play a *very* limited number of high-margin roles within it. Pepsi targeted the whole food and drinks sector and played a wide range of roles all with different margin potential.

What all of this means for us is that our principles of atomization have a first class precedent. Eschewing contemporary trends for vertical integration and direct involvement with the physical product, from very early in its history, Coke saw the value of operating as a small, smart molecule in a vast and atomized space.

RISE AND FALL OF THE VERTICAL MARKETPLACE

Emergence of the vertical

Marketplaces and e-procurement projects are not easy to implement. For one thing, it is not always easy to persuade the suppliers to play ball. They must codify their goods and produce electronic catalogues, a costly and time-consuming business.

With two or more large players within an industry facing the same problem, one answer often adopted was to combine their cataloguing needs and "persuade" their shared suppliers to co-operate. This precipitated the birth of the vertical marketplace – a place where corporations could find information on suppliers of indirect goods, perhaps placing the order using a shared e-procurement system.

The founders soon realized that other organizations within the industry would be attracted by easy access to catalogues, and that transaction fees from these new participants would produce a bounty. Predictions were made of astronomical market capitalizations for these marketplaces, and the gold rush was on. Soon almost every industry had marketplaces competing for the attention of suppliers and for the business of the large buyers.

Death of the vertical

At the end of 1999, there were perhaps 100 Internet-based marketplaces in existence, mostly horizontal. One year later, there were hundreds of vertical marketplaces in existence with thousands more planned.

But we think that by the end of 2004 most of these vertical marketplaces will have collapsed or changed roles. There is just not enough indirect procurement to go round to support all of these marketplaces. At the start of this decade, transaction charges within competing steel marketplaces were already less than one percent, and many commentators expect transaction charges in all marketplaces to drop effectively to zero. Many of the vertical marketplaces that have been banking on high and sustained income from transactions will run out of cash, forcing the backers to decide whether to plough more money into an unsuccessful business or to cut their losses.

Lack of liquidity is bad enough, but we think there is a more fundamental reason why many of these vertical marketplaces will fail – their concentration on indirect goods. Sustained value to a business can only come from identifying what is wrong with its principal processes and then fixing it, and the remaining problems lie in the sea of inefficiency between the corporations. Indirect procurement is, at best, tinkering in the margins.

Forrester Research[3] predict that only 181 marketplaces will succeed in the USA – that's 181 out of thousands announced. Worldwide figures will be higher, but the B2C shakeout of 2000–2001 will look like a minor event compared to the B2B marketplace collapses of 2001–2003.

Just as corporations have to adapt to face changes in customer demand and respond to the challenges of lower transaction costs, so marketplaces will have to change.

The future of the vertical?

We think the true role for a vertical marketplace is to move away from indirect procurement and provide a mechanism for collaboration and process standardization within the industry.

Ford emerges having shown considerable vision. When it announced its vertical marketplace early in 2000 the aim was not to automate indirect procurement but to standardize the supply chain and to provide a development environment where dealers, suppliers and Ford's engineers could get together to collaborate on the design of the next generation of Ford's vehicles. Far from coincidentally, General Motors also announced a more traditional e-procurement-based vertical on the same day. But it soon became clear that having two sets of standards within the industry would not be tolerated by the suppliers. So the marketplaces merged in February 2000 to form Covisint.

The aim of Covisint,[4] apart from streamlining the industry's procurement methods, is to allow collaborative production planning and scheduling and to eliminate some of the inventory in the supply chain, which constitutes 10–15 percent of the automotive industry's annual sales. But even the trailblazing Covisint is not perfect – two of the largest automotive manufacturers, Volkswagen and BMW,[5] have refused to participate openly fearing that their trade secrets will be violated.

Everyone wins if these marketplaces provide a mechanism that makes real the visibility up and down the value chain that EDI promised but never delivered. There is real value in providing an industrial facilitation mechanism where buyers, suppliers, customers and competitors can join hands to identify problem areas in the industry and solve them to the benefit of all. This sounds cosy and altruistic, but it goes well beyond that. If 10–15 percent of an industry's total sales are tied up in inventory, it is a reasonable bet that the total cost of supply chain inefficiency will be closer to 25–30 percent. The benefits of ensuring better information flow will be huge.

This type of vertical will take time to form even though its immediate advantages are clear. For starters, it needs to be built around a completely different kind of software than existing vertical marketplaces. Some or these verticals will effectively be "private," dominated by one corporation,[6] while others will stress their neutrality, working to create independent industry standards.[7]

FALL AND RISE OF THE HORIZONTAL MARKETPLACE

As we said at the start of the chapter, most of the early marketplaces were horizontal – offering a single process (usually indirect procurement) that spanned industry boundaries. These marketplaces were crushed, or at least bruised, as larger corporations realized the value of their buying power and rushed into vertical marketplaces. We think the tide will turn, and horizontals will re-emerge, albeit in a different form.

COVISINT

Covisint began as an attempt on the part of Ford and General Motors to exploit the potential of the Internet to reduce costs. In just two years, it has grown into a significant force that could change the entire structure of the industry. If it realizes its potential to transfer real-time information between key partners in the auto industry it will have an industry-wide impact on product development, worldwide procurement and supply-chain co-ordination.

This will give automobile manufacturers the potential to speed up the process of vehicle design from the current cycle of 3–4 years to 12–18 months. They have the capability to develop true build-to-order systems, enabling a customer to receive the specific car they order rather than taking one off the dealer's lot.

In 1999, Ford and General Motors had separate plans to develop procurement sites on the Internet, to lower the costs of bought-in components and deliver savings. They decided to merge their sites and invited other automakers to join. DaimlerChrysler signed up in February 2000 and the Renault-Nissan alliance in April 2000. The first transaction was completed in October 2000 and it became the largest B2B marketplace (in terms of transactions) in just three months.

E-procurement will realize significant savings over traditional procurement systems, but what sets Covisint apart from other B2B exchanges is its networking of different actors within the automotive value chain to bring substantial shifts in the way the industry works.

In product development, Covisint will assist in real-time collaboration between component suppliers and automakers, and within the automakers' own organizations, to bring vehicle designs to market quicker.

Finally in supply-chain management, Covisint will provide forecasting and planning tools as well as facilitating real-time inventory management, reducing waste and stocks and providing real savings to automakers.

In essence, Covisint is taking all of the business innovations of the last decade – just-in-time inventory management, order-to-delivery systems and cross-functional product development teams, and combining them in a powerful e-enabling function.

Just as it makes sense to us to use vertical marketplaces to specialize in improving the supply chain (i.e. direct goods), so it makes sense to put indirect procurement through horizontal marketplaces. The competencies that corporations need to buy indirect items efficiently (e.g. negotiation and supplier development skills) are *process*-based and are broadly the same regardless of the item being purchased or the industry involved. These competencies can be better developed in a horizontal marketplace, where economies of scale can be developed with a lesser chance of regulatory disruption.[8]

Specialist procurement – for direct items and a small proportion of unique indirect items – may well stay in the verticals, but we think that corporations will eventually gravitate towards horizontal marketplaces to source the majority of their indirect goods.

MARKETPLACES IN AN ATOMIC WORLD

Vertical marketplaces become communications channels

If our atoms are to thrive, they need an environment where transaction costs will be permanently low. The connectivity created by vertical marketplaces, whether private marketplaces tied to the large manufacturers or public marketplaces acting as low-cost communications channels, provides that environment.

The vertical marketplaces will be built on top of asset platform atoms, just as they are currently created by industry "gorillas." Our version of a marketplace like Covisint would contain customer managers or webspinners channeling the demand through to the asset platforms which assemble vehicles, while smart companies work together to design the next generation of vehicles.

But what about industry-wide processes? Is there not a role for someone to manage functions such as warehousing, inventory management, reduction of surplus capacity in the asset base, supplier certification, catalogue management, and specialist training? Of course there is. We think these processes will be managed as a profitable business by service platforms, initially via the sponsors of the private marketplaces but increasingly as independent businesses.

Horizontal marketplaces become service platforms

And in addition to just bringing suppliers and buyers together, there is a real opportunity for horizontal marketplaces to create liquidity by co-ordinating buying or selling activities. Over time, these marketplaces will take on more and more of the generic processes until they become indistinguishable from service platform atoms. The CoNext case study below demonstrates one such evolution.

CONEXT

The more you can aggregate buying power, the better the prices you can get from your suppliers. Buying clubs, where organizations offer their best procurement deals to other organizations, are decades old, but in 1999 supply-chain specialists A.T. Kearney saw an opportunity in the rise of digital marketplaces. Mike Jacobs, a vice-president at A.T. Kearney explains: "The horizontal marketplaces at the time had broad catalogues but the deals in them were not that good – nobody had introduced good sourcing disciplines like reducing the number of suppliers or consolidating spend. Whereas the buying clubs, some of which we had set up, had not taken advantage of the lower transaction costs [brought about by] marketplaces."

The result was CoNext, a joint venture between A.T. Kearney and its parent company EDS, targeted at large multinational corporations. Customers were asked to pass control over an element of their procurement spend to professional buyers with deep experience of that category. Although the customers would lose an element of control over purchasing, they would obtain superb prices, and transaction costs would be kept low by access to a shared e-procurement system. Twelve large corporations soon signed up, and benefits were indeed delivered.

CoNext, like all of the horizontal marketplaces, suffered from the rush to the verticals. But it is an early example of a service platform and its value proposition will remain strong while that of the verticals declines. CoNext, or son-of-CoNext, will rise again.

Webspinners link marketplaces

At the moment, vertical marketplaces work within the industry's current supply chains. In future, webspinners will exist partly to introduce new blood into the value chain and partly to co-ordinate services that cross industry boundaries which need to be assembled for a particular customer offer. The webspinner forges the relationship; the marketplace(s) makes the communications work.

Sometimes, the webspinner may arbitrate between industries. Consider the case of today's customer with no means of transport. If you work in the automotive industry, you'll probably want to sell the guy a vehicle. If you are a finance house you will want to arrange a finance deal for him so that he can buy it, and perhaps sell him some insurance.

But what he wants (as you would have found out if you had taken the trouble to ask him) is a way of moving his family and goods about the landscape with certain guarantees of availability, reliability, safety and comfort. The components of the offer (the vehicle, the finance and the insurance) are secondary to this.

Sure, the transportation need as communicated by the customer manager could be met by owning a vehicle, in which case the webspinner will search for the best finance and insurance deals. But the best solution for him might be a rent-it-when-you-need-it deal from a service platform involved in aggregating car rental demand and providing global rental services. Both of these options meet the customer's need, but they provide different combinations of availability, flexibility and cost.

Either way, our customer will need fuel, so we would expect the webspinner to look for a guaranteed rate for the next three years from a service platform specializing in commodity futures.

WORKING IN A MOLECULAR ECONOMY

Finally, let's take a look at how the atoms will change the economic world around us.

Globalization

Periodically, the streets in the western world are filled with demonstrators protesting against the rise of global corporations. We think both these protestors and the corporations' shareholders will probably prefer our molecular economy.

Most of the atom types will be small, with lower transaction costs providing more opportunity for local providers to exploit niches in the economy. This provides opportunities for, say, a smart company based in India to do business with the American market (via customer managers such as Yahoo! or AOL), possibly via a European webspinner.

Service platforms will probably be specific to a particular geography (for example, there are vast differences between employment and tax laws in Europe and the United States, and there would be little benefit in running a process-specific business that crosses the Atlantic). The exception to globalization will be the asset platforms, which may well be organized globally to achieve economies of scale.

Taxation and regulation

Service and asset platforms, by their nature, have a *permanent establishment* in a particular territory and will be bound by the laws and taxation systems of that territory. Webspinners and customer managers have no such restrictions. Although there are benefits to a physical base, their communications with their customers and suppliers can be entirely virtual. This means that for industries that deliver virtual products – gambling, entertainment, information, financial services – taxation and regulation will become increasingly difficult as they lose their structure.

International taxation authorities are only just beginning to wake up to the power of the Internet to sell things (the rest of us found that out in 1995) and they are years away from developing structures which adequately tax and regulate virtual corporations, yet alone shifting groups of atoms.

A NEW PERIODIC TABLE

We are now in a position where we can complete our chemical analogy. In the material world, molecules with different characteristics (plastics, glass, liquids, gases, enzymes, proteins, DNA etc.) fill different roles within our environment. All of these molecules are formed by atoms bonding with other types of atoms (by exchanging electrons through special bond orbitals). The physical properties of the atoms are described in chemical shorthand as "elements."

Dimitri Ivanovich Mendeleev described how all of the elements fell into families by laying them out in his periodic table – each column describing a different family where the elements showed similar bond-forming behavior.

In the periodic table that describes our new economy, we have families of atoms with exotic new names (customer managers, webspinners etc.). Within the families we will see similarities (e.g. procurement service platforms and HR service platforms), and the atoms will create bonds with other atoms by exchanging transactions through marketplaces. Just as in the physical world, some of these bonds are temporary while others are longer lasting, and many of the bonds are created by catalysts (webspinners).

Don't be fooled by the 100-odd elements. Only twenty or so of them really matter, and this leads to the infinite diversity of the physical world around us. While we only have six atoms types, we hope you look forward with us to the economic diversity that will be created by the molecular economy.

Regulation is another thorny issue. Take the banking industry, for example. As it fragments into customer managers, transaction-processing service platforms, and specialist smart companies, how is each part to be regulated?

Virtual enterprises can effectively only be regulated by customer pressure. Remember that we are talking about a world where information is visible, where customers can rate each interaction with a supplier and make that rating brutally obvious to the world. In fact, we see this "provision of transparency" as being one of the main functions of webspinners and customer managers.

Another side effect of an atomizing world is the ability to manipulate transfer pricing. Where different business units within a corporation perform services for each other, as they will in a company going through the process of atomization, profits can be taken in parts of the world which have low-tax or no-tax regimes. Consider an atomizing pharmaceutical corporation – it can place its manufacturing atoms in countries with high taxes but low labor costs, and its research facilities (its smart companies) in countries with low corporate taxation. Since, crudely speaking, profit accrues at the point where the risk was taken, corporations can minimize their overall tax bill.

The tax authorities and regulators will catch on, and the situation will eventually change,[9] but it may be two decades before the situation stabilizes. But until then, opportunities abound.

SUMMARY

Atoms and marketplaces may be individually small and incomplete, but they can combine into systems that are powerful, fast and immensely flexible, and still manage to completely meet customer expectations.

Individuals will form alliances with customer managers that really understand them, and that provide the conduit through which they can express their needs, using any and all channels available to them. Webspinners create the packages to satisfy those needs by forming alliances in real-time, from elements from within or across industries. Specialist design and consultancy shops provide the innovation that keeps the economy going, and a few giants of global scope concentrate on production.

It would be premature to describe the development of vertical and horizontal marketplaces as complete. But they have begun to take a form that we think will be recognizable in years to come. We think they will play an important part in driving the atomization of corporations as well as in defining the future structures of the new atomic entities.

The successful vertical marketplaces of the future will be the ones that offer more than just the initial cost benefits of aggregated demand. They will succeed because they offer an environment in which supply chain participants can collaborate to their mutual benefit. This will ultimately be most relevant to direct purchasing requirements, leaving plenty of room for a re-emergence of horizontal marketplaces to more efficiently service the indirect requirements.

CHAPTER 9

Atomizing the Corporation

INTRODUCTION

A TOMIC CORPORATIONS HAVE a number of clear advantages. They are small enough to be efficient *and* agile, and as part of a network of other tightly-targeted organizations they have access to a range of skills that they need not possess in-house.

All organizations, atomic or monolithic, will see rapid drops in external transaction cost but these superbly streamlined atoms will, by their nature, have low internal transaction costs as well. The molecules will out-compete large, vertically-integrated corporations, and the future for the giants is clear. They must themselves deconstruct, atomize, and focus.

We've said before that some of the players that will dominate the new economy will come from today's large corporations, and that some will not. Many of today's large corporations will transform and survive, many will struggle and perish. The next decade will brutally punish the mediocre. In the words of Evans and Wurster, authors of *Blown to Bits*, "Deconstruction is most likely to strike in precisely those parts of the business where incumbents have most to lose and are least willing to recognize it."[1]

If you are a leader within a current corporation, you will probably be involved in decisions about its future shape. If you have got this far in the book (thanks again!) you may well feel apprehensive, because the shape of your current employer almost certainly does not match the picture of the economy we have created. Your will probably be asking:

■ What should we concentrate on?
■ What do we retain?

- What should we do with the rest of the corporation?
- What are the atoms worth?
- How big are they?
- Which parts can we extract value from and which should we simply ditch?

We hope to answer those questions in this chapter and the next, which are aimed at those planning (or is it plotting?) atomization of their corporation. After a description of how large corporations are constructed, we will look at two ways of identifying atoms hidden in your corporation – the first by layer and the second by a detailed examination of its components. The next chapter looks at the composition and valuation of the atoms. A word of caution: don't imagine for one moment that atomization will be painless. It is inconceivable that so much energy and value could be released without some collateral damage. But that should not be used as an excuse to defer the inevitable. Atomization is the only effective response to the changing environment – trying to hang on to the status quo will be the surest guarantee of terminal decline.

WHAT ARE CORPORATIONS MADE OF?

We need to take a look at the components of today's corporation, not in terms of geographic boundaries or the strategic business units (SBUs) that they choose to organize themselves into, but in terms of the value that the parts add to each other and to the shareholders.

We would like you to think of a corporation as an apple sliced into layers, as demonstrated in Fig. 9.1. We accept that some organizations might not possess all of these layers, but let's be complete.

Governance

Where do we find the core, or perhaps the soul, of a large corporation? It isn't in the units that make the products of the corporation, or in the layers of middle management. Generally these are focused on output (or politics) and are the

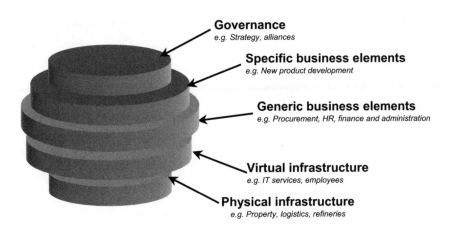

Governance
e.g. Strategy, alliances

Specific business elements
e.g. New product development

Generic business elements
e.g. Procurement, HR, finance and administration

Virtual infrastructure
e.g. IT services, employees

Physical infrastructure
e.g. Property, logistics, refineries

Fig. 9.1 Layers of the corporation.

tools by which strategy is implemented, rather than being part of the strategy-setting process.

We argue that the core of even the largest corporation is probably not more than 10–100 people who perform the governance functions of the corporation. These functions consist of strategy, oversight and alliance management.

■ Corporate strategy consists of deciding why the corporation exists, what it will set out to do and, in the broadest terms, how to do it.

■ Oversight ensures, with the lightest touch possible, delivery of the strategy. This is perhaps the least of the three functions: day-to-day operational details (quite rightly) rarely intrude into this level except where decisions on corporate policy are needed.

■ Management of strategic alliances and relationships involves the control of relations with a few key stakeholders, such as major investors, governments, sometimes the trades unions, and with key business partners.

Specific business elements

The next layer of our apple contains things that differentiate our corporation from its peers. These elements are the ones which make a positive difference to the success of the corporation. They may be obvious to all (think of Coca-Cola's famous "secret recipe" and the marketing which promotes it), or far more subtle (Wal-Mart's excellence in supplier management, or Cisco's virtual manufacturing processes).

What these differentiators are will vary from industry to industry, but one would commonly see items such as:

- *process knowledge* – how to build that better mousetrap, or how to make the same mousetrap better than your competitors;
- *knowledge processes* – processes to generate and harvest knowledge;
- *product specifications and design* (think Coca-Cola);
- *intellectual property* – management of specific items of knowledge or expertise (e.g mathematical understanding of stock markets, drugs, patents etc.);
- *human inventory* – in some industries, the staff of the organization constitute its products, for example in academia, journalism, consultancies, merchant banking, advertising and other forms of prostitution;
- *brand management*, especially for consumer products corporations; and
- *good relationships*, either with customers or within supply chains.

Generic business elements

The majority of the processes that the corporation performs will be generic – you would find the same processes in their competitors, and probably even in different industries.

These processes or elements are often used to operate the corporation rather than contribute towards its products. All corporations have at least one procurement function, at least one HR function, at least one IT function etc.

The role of these functions is hardly ever strategic to the corporation, despite what they tell the CEO during the budget allocation cycle! They rarely make an outstandingly positive contribution to success because there is so little room for them to differentiate the corporation or add real value to it. That is not to say that these functions can be ignored – disastrous marketing, lousy IT or sloppy cash management can kill a corporation faster than poor strategic vision.

There are some exceptions to the rule that generic functions are not differentiators. Wal-Mart's supplier management processes and IT in the wholesale banking industry are clearly major contributors to the corporation's success. So much so, that in these cases we would generally promote the elements to the layer above.

But most corporations tolerate the resources that these generic macroprocesses consume because they are "just part of doing business." Let's look at the following examples.

- *Finance and accounting*. Cash and treasury management, accounts payable and receivable processes, financial reporting etc., are processes that all corporations carry out, with the underlying processes so similar that they are often externally regulated. Professional services such as tax and legal advice would also fall into this layer.
- *Information technology*. While the types of systems that IT functions produce differ from industry to industry, the processes that are used to produce them are generally pretty similar.
- *Human relations*. Recruitment and retention of staff, benefits management (including payroll), health & safety, discipline and firing, etc. These processes tend to differ by geography rather than by industry.

Virtual infrastructure

In this layer we find "fixed" infrastructure items that are used to support the generic processes of the business, such as office space, computer and communications hardware and software. Unlike the capital assets of the business, managers see the virtual infrastructure as ancillary to the operations of the corporation and are willing to take make-or-buy decisions on where it comes from.

For most corporations, the exceptions being the "human inventory" professions listed above, we would also include the workforce in this layer as it carries out relatively fixed tasks which are often closely related to the fixed assets of the corporation. Sufficient numbers of people, with sufficient training, could deliver the same results regardless of whether they were contractors or permanent employees. Of course, it matters to the employees (that's why we have labor laws) but to the employer the question is again one of the balance between internal and external costs. So management makes rent-or-hire decisions where the workforce is concerned. Temporary hires are no longer restricted to typists and administrative support, and there are some industries (healthcare, construction) where the workforce feels more allegiance to the profession as a whole than to any particular employer.

Physical infrastructure

Most corporations, with the exception of those purely in the service industries, have considerable amounts of capital in physical infrastructure – assembly lines, refineries, trucks, warehouses etc. In some industries, the profitability of the business is almost entirely based on this layer. Corporations in these industries tend to use principal performance measures related to the assets – such as Mean Time Between Failures, Production Output, Return on Investment, or Return on Capital Employed – and are often characterized by good profit margins and low P/E ratios.

ATOMIZATION BY LAYER

In a few paragraphs, we will restate what should be obvious to you by now as to the source of the atoms. Before then, we want to attack the popular notion that corporations have to be self-sufficient.

As we have discussed, physical capital is diminishing in terms of its importance to the share price, and the new sources of value come from intangible and relational capital.

We are facing a time of competition and opportunity that exceeds anything we have seen in the last five decades, and this is the right time for CEOs to examine everything that their corporation does. The questions to ask are *what?* and *how?*

Let's get back to the basics of the corporation. If an asset or a process represents what the corporation does, then it should be retained. If it repre-

THE ASSET TRAP

If questioned, most traditional managers in these corporations would see these physical things as their strategic assets and as barriers to entry for the competition. There is some truth in this view, but only some. Capital assets certainly can be the strategic base of the corporation, if the corporation does not fool itself that it is customer-focused. And yes, capital assets certainly are barriers to entry – building them requires considerable access to funds and expertise in their design and operation. More importantly though, they are barriers to change, because they impose an inflexible mindset on the corporation and make it concentrate on its operations rather than its customers.

Consider the store chains where every store is laid out according to the same pattern, or railway networks that still follow the same routes that were laid out a century ago. Sure, it is efficient, but is it what the customer wants? Asset-laden corporations, in our experience, often have no means of answering this question or often of seeing beyond the asset base.

The consequences of the asset trap are serious – concentration on your means of production rather than on your customers means increasing commoditization, decreasing price, and squeezed margins. Being the lowest-cost provider of commodities can be very profitable and we are not saying that it is a *bad* place to be (someone needs to do it), but the declining market capitalizations that go with it do not sit well with most CEOs or shareholders.

sents something that is part of *how* it does, then it should not be the focus of your scarce management attention and can be sold or scrapped (Fig. 9.2).

This is a radical vision – to accept it means that corporations must ask themselves what it is that they, and only they, do best, and then letting go of everything else. Every corporation has things that it does – things that it has to do – that it does not care about. Reductions in external transaction costs means that it is possible to unbundle these things from the corporation, either as a source of (relational) capital worth or as a potential cost saving. Either way, we see this as the final nail in the coffin of self-sufficiency.

Core to business

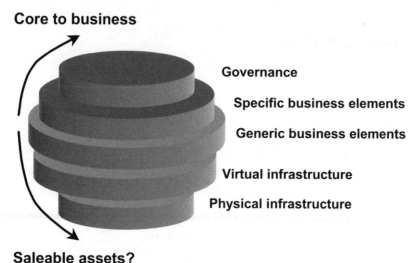

Governance

Specific business elements

Generic business elements

Virtual infrastructure

Physical infrastructure

Saleable assets?

Fig. 9.2 Unbundling the generic.

Let's use an example. It is entirely possible that you may own one too many refineries, or you have the area's best-run HR department. These are untapped sources of capital, and you can make use of these assets by floating them off as a separate business, either retained under your control, or used as a cash generator via an IPO.

If your HR department is *not* the best in the area, then maybe there is a corporation nearby with a better one. Coming to an arrangement with them could reduce your fixed costs and increase services to the employees (making you, in turn, more productive). Under either situation, everyone wins (except the worst of the two HR departments).

Similarly, a chemicals corporation could concentrate on production, or it could concentrate instead on specific business processes, such as managing the feedstocks and routes to market, or maintaining a research team and a set of protected intellectual property. Even this set of assets can be contracted if necessary – the corporation could for example subcontract its research if it is not an industry leader!

So, to the re-statement of the obvious. You will almost certainly have figured out how our potential atom types correspond to the layers of the corporation:

- the physical infrastructure layer, if you have it, will clearly become a set of asset-based business platforms;
- the virtual infrastructure and generic process layers will become, or be replaced by, service platforms;
- specific business elements, if they truly have the power to differentiate, will be the basis of a valuable smart company, webspinner or customer manager; and
- the governance layer will be the core of a portfolio owner that retains a financial stake in the other atoms.

Figure 9.3 demonstrates how a typical corporation might split, with atoms derived from specific business elements, each with a small governance layer, floating on a sea of lower-level platforms.

HUNTING FOR ATOMS

Identifying the elements of complex corporations

It is not always possible to divide corporations into these neat layers and in most cases a bottom-up approach to identification will be needed. Here is an

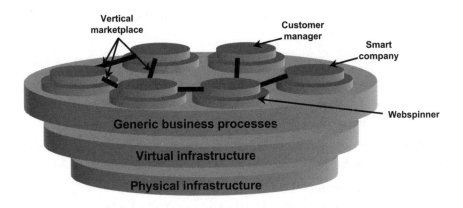

Fig. 9.3   Atoms on a sea of platforms.

exercise you can go through to help you find the atoms within your corporation by looking at your corporation in terms of its low-level structure.

Perhaps the best place to start is with the organization chart, although it rarely describes the myriad functions of the business units and often combines or omits support processes. To find the atoms by this route, you will need to identify each of these supporting elements.

Here is a good method of developing a checklist of potential atoms to add to the organization chart:

■ Write down everything your company does, avoiding general phrases like "services" or general sector descriptions like "retail banking" or "tele-communications." Replace the generalizations with specifics: try to use verbs and nouns that describe specific things that you do for the customer. Avoid small distinctions between products (such as two chemicals produced by the same process or two types of insurance product).

■ Imagine that you will fire everyone that doesn't directly deliver those things, then count off the products or services that you can't deliver any longer. This will give you a few more things you need to add to the list from the first step.

You now have either a revised organization chart or a simple list of potential atoms, and the next step is to decide which atom type they fit into and whether they could survive as a viable atom. Figure 9.4 shows an idealized organization structure, which we will use for the purposes of demonstration.

Atomic analysis

We take that next step, for each potential atom, by working though the following sets of questions, labelled a–e, and assessing which group of answers puts the potential atom in the best light. It is pretty obvious which atom types correspond to which group of questions, so we will label them for your convenience.

And this is no time for rose-tinted spectacles. Be absolutely honest. Think how a liquidator would look at the business if it had to be suddenly shut down.

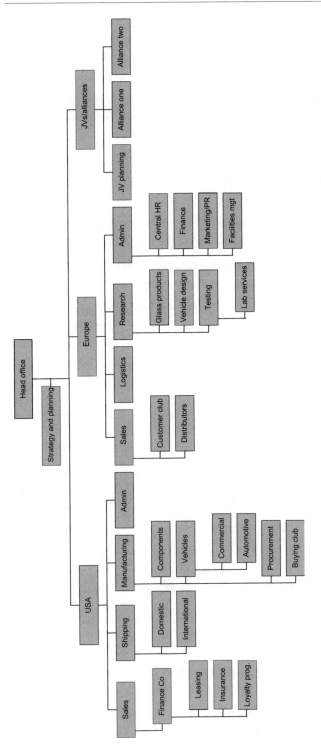

Fig. 9.4 Organization chart for Monolith, Inc.

Customer manager

a   Can you say, honestly, that everything this part of the corporation does adds direct value to your customers? (And yes, we mean everything). How do you measure that value?

a   Is the price the customer pays related to the value he perceives, or to the cost base of this atom?

a   How do customers perceive the value of your brand? Is it *really* worth anything to them? If this atom disappeared from the market, could they find alternative products?

a   How well do you know the customer here? We don't mean numbers or segments, but names, education, lifestage, leisure activities, ambitions, and desires ...

a   Do you have a single record of a customer's every interaction with you, and how they felt about you during it?

a   What gives you the right to own part of the customer's lifestyle?

a   Do you try to fit your customers to your products, or your products to your customers? (Be honest).

Webspinner

b   Do you control any alliances that define the shape of the industry (think Microsoft and Intel)? Do your competitors?

b   Can you quantify the value of your alliances?

c   Is there a formal alliance management process? How many days does the process take? (Sorry, did you just say *months*?) Is there a formal alliance dissolution process?

b   Do you know everyone in your industry, globally, and their strengths and weaknesses?

b   Would you say that most of the employees of this atom could set up their own successful businesses if they had to?

Smart company

c   Do you consistently out-innovate your competitors, or would you say you are a fast follower?

c   How many days does it take to bring a new product to market? How much faster is this than the competition?

c   Do you provide consultancy services in their purest form (regardless of the industry)?

c   Are you world-class at capturing or sharing knowledge, or are you in an environment where knowledge is regarded as power?

c   What steps do you take to protect your best ideas while making them publicly available?

c   Would the majority of your employees have college degrees or equivalent technical/artistic qualifications?

c   Is this part of your corporation renowned for ideas, intellect, and creativity?

Service platform

d   Are your internal process good? *Really* good?

d   Do you provide process- or infrastructure-based services to others? (By this, we mean generic business processes such as accounting or IT outsourcing, or equipment or property leasing).

d   Do your clients tend to work mostly for one industry, or are they spread across a variety of sectors?

d   Would a massive increase in scale increase the efficiency and quality of your processes and operations, or would it make them massively worse?

Asset platform

e   Are these production units the best, fastest or cheapest in the business?

e   Do you think that barriers to entry in your industry are high? Are they mostly based on capital investment?

e   Do you feel that your share price is based on a fair reflection of the tangible assets of the company?

e   If you had to choose between operational excellence or agility, would you plump for excellence?

When you have worked through all parts of the organization and grouped them into potential atoms, your chart perhaps looking something like the worked example in Fig. 9.5.

You may often come up with a complex answer, perhaps feeling that several of the descriptions matched your potential atom. If that is the case, then

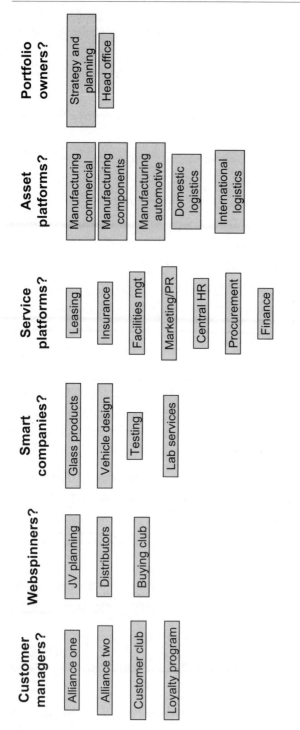

Fig. 9.5 Potential atom types from Monolith, Inc.

you are either not being honest with yourself or you need to break the organizational unit into smaller parts and repeat the exercise.

If you finished the exercise feeling depressed and without a single positive response, then you are either not being honest about your employer's abilities or should find a new company, preferably today.

REPLICATING THE CORPORATION

Sketch the new corporation

So by the end of the preceding exercise, you should have a list of atoms concealed in your organization, a potential goldmine of locked-up relational capital.

While we are advocating the atomization of the current corporation, that does not mean its obliteration. The current organization exists for a purpose. You will remember that in Chapter 2 we said that businesses exist to convert inputs (raw materials, knowledge, labor) into more valuable outputs (products, services etc.). Presumably, the market still has a need for those outputs, and the next step is to work out how they will continue to be created by the corporation in its new atomized form.

For each of the atoms, try to list its inputs and outputs. Then, starting from the "output" end of the existing corporation, try to sketch out the molecules that will be used to create the output, remembering that some of the services might be sourced from outside in future. Think about how each of the atoms will source its inputs and distribute its outputs.

This sketch of how the atoms fit together, and how they fit into the molecular economy, should help to convince you that the deconstructed corporation is workable. Figure 9.6 is one solution corresponding to our worked example above. You will notice that the grouped boxes in the figure correspond to the layers described at the start of this chapter.

And question the current structure

The final step of the process is to compare the sketch of the atomized corpora-

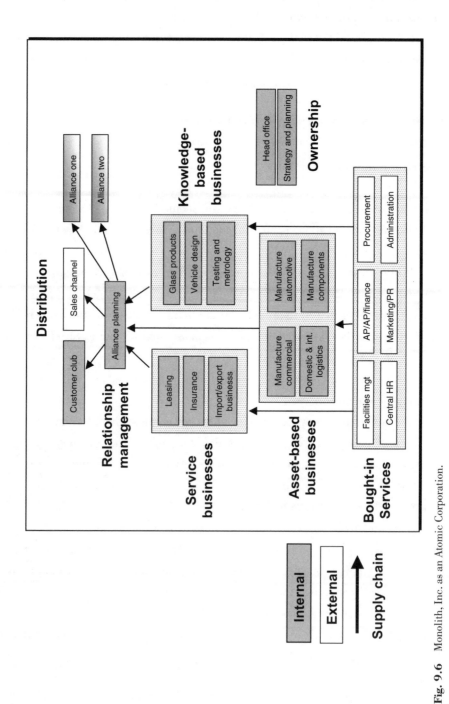

Fig. 9.6 Monolith, Inc. as an Atomic Corporation.

tion against its current structure, especially if your corporation is currently arranged as a set of vertical silos, for example as quasi-independent strategic business units.

If the sketch of the atoms aligns neatly to the existing internal structure, then the atomization process will be relatively easy, as the SBUs can be considered and atomized independently.

Unfortunately, it's just as likely that your new sketch ignored your SBU boundaries. This is a more difficult situation to unpick (especially while maintaining some semblance of "business as usual"), but it's imperative that you do so as you have just demonstrated that your SBU structure is not viable in anything other than the short term.

But whatever the shape of the new corporation, the next step in the process is to work out how we get to there from here, by thinking about the composition of the atoms and generating an outline business plan for each of the individual atoms. That's what we will handle in the next chapter.

SUMMARY

Atomization is a root and branch process. Nothing is left unexamined. And if it emerges that something can be done better elsewhere then it is time to accept the reality of the connected economy. There is value for you in transferring some of your functions into expert hands. But if you don't produce a baldly honest sketch of how your existing corporation functions then the eventual process of atomization won't do justice to the components.

This chapter should have prepared the groundwork for reorienting the atoms into the molecules that will ensure sustainable success in the marketplace. The next stage is to assess their worth and explore the process of putting them together.

CHAPTER 10

Atomic Numbers

INTRODUCTION

WE HAVE EXPLAINED the theory of atomization but have not yet focused on the practicalities of what it means for future corporations. This chapter will address questions about the sort of skill sets that people will need in the different atoms, what sort of management they will require, what will happen to things like corporate brand, and what the atoms will be worth.

That last question may be the most important of all. It is not going to be easy to set the process in train without the endorsement of shareholders. And we will progress to proposing some ways to develop an outline business plan for each of the atoms.

RUNNING THE ATOMS

How big are the atoms?

Asset platforms will usually be fairly large, because they will need access to capital. But what about these other types?

All atoms need a vision and that implies, in the terminology of the last chapter, a governance layer. So, clearly, the smallest possible size for an atom is one person. This is not realistic, of course.

Atomic size is determined by the now familiar equation, the balance between co-ordination and transaction costs. While such a tiny atom would have internal transaction costs of nearly zero, the cost of doing business externally is likely to be much higher, especially in the early years of this decade. So while we would expect atoms to gradually shrink with time, they may start off reasonably large.

How large is reasonably large? Here's an exercise that should give you a rough target payroll for each of the atoms. For each of the atoms that you identified in the last chapter, identify the minimum number of people that are directly associated with it. We have to ask you to be brutally honest again, taking out all of the secretaries, janitors, management, and people associated with the generic processes. The resulting total will be quite a small number, and probably too small to run the atom effectively. So we will need to add a few people (let's say 10 percent) for strategy and governance and a few more (perhaps another 20 percent) to handle getting the business and making sure the company runs – it is this latter number that will shrink most over the decade.

We estimate that for most atoms this total figure will be closer to 100 people than 1000. The payroll of the large asset platforms and the service-based horizontals may be measured in the low thousands, and we would expect these to be created by mergers from current businesses.

Under any circumstances that we can think of, the new corporations will be much smaller than the current Fortune Global 100, where payrolls of 100,000–300,000 are typical.

Sharing the benefits

If you are going through this exercise because you are planning for atomization, this is the time to show prudence. If you talk publicly of turning the large and comfortable "mother ship" into a set of small and lean units, you will almost certainly unleash a great deal of skepticism, fear and hostility from within the existing business. There are corporations even today where the majority of senior executives have been on the payroll for more than thirty years, and you can expect the resistance from these veterans to be particularly intense.

But don't let any nervousness put you off embarking on this task. We really are not talking about shedding 99 percent plus of the payroll (and you most certainly should not!). A much better way of approaching the atomization of the business is to view it as the unlocking of a set of huge opportunities for the shareholders, the workforce and the customers.

Your shareholders should benefit the most. Although they lose direct control over the assets of the corporation, they gain a stake in the resulting atoms via the portfolio owner that we would expect to evolve from the governance layer. And as we will show later in this chapter, we would certainly expect the sum of the values of the atoms to exceed the value of the parent corporation.

While many of the old-timers may regret or resist atomization, we believe that there will be at least as many employees that welcome it. This proportion can be increased by giving a share of the released value of the atoms to its employees and management – there should still be more than sufficient relational capital generated to compensate the shareholders for the loss of the assets and income under direct control.

Your customers will benefit as well. It will feel as if they are dealing with both a small company and a large one. The small company will be the atom, which because it is concentrating on doing one or two things very well, will be *very* responsive to the customers' needs. But there should also be the sensation of dealing with a large company because of the range of products and services and the depth of competence that are behind the atom, delivered through a web of alliances.

Who manages the atoms?

The next job for the planner is to consider the skills portfolio needed to make the atom work as a separate business, as well as the exact ownership split and governance structure of the atoms. Is there an identifiable management team for the atom? Is it part of the current management structure? Are they entrepreneurial enough?

The skills that will be needed to manage the atom's future (managing customers, managing knowledge and managing relationships) are *not* the same as those needed to survive as middle-to-upper management in a large corporation (which often seem to be managing the complexity of the organization, budgeting, and politics). And many of today's managers will need to rethink their value proposition.

This may sometimes present you, the planner, with some interesting issues on where the management team will come from. In some cases, there even may be no viable in-house management team, especially in corporations where staff turnover is low, and it may be time to think of a management buy-in.

But most of the time, we think it is likely that you will find that the potential atoms are full of star performers with ideas as to how the business could be improved, if only you got out of their way!

But whatever the origin of the identified management team, let them now take a look at the proposed atom and suggest some changes. If the proposed governance structure is right, they stand to profit from a successful business venture, so let them identify where they could cut costs to increase its viability, and how they would decommoditize it a little[1] to increase the attractiveness of a trading relationship with the rest of the corporation.

Where will you find specialist skills?

We explained above that the kind of skills needed to manage the atomic version of the corporation may not be the same as those needed to manage its current incarnation. Unlike the large corporations, which favor generalists and often try to cultivate them by moving staff around between dissimilar posts every couple of years, atoms will require specific skills.

How specific? One of the oldest maxims of economics is that "the division of labour is limited by the extent of the market."[2] This means that the likely size of the audience determines the degree to which the players can afford to specialize. Think of the variety of specialist restaurants in a city as compared to a small town. And since the new Web-enabled global market is very large, we would expect considerable specialization among the atoms that service it.

The competencies that such atoms will need are considered in Table 10.1.

Table 10.1 Specialist skills by atom type.

Customer managers	Marketing, particular "life need" experience (e.g. employment, parenting, learning), consumer interaction skills (e.g. anthropology, design), data mining, knowledge management.
Webspinners	Ability to form relationships, broad range of contacts, alliance management, legal expertise, collaboration.
Service platform	Process expertise, efficiency focus, probably considerable IT skills.
Asset platform	Industry expertise, asset management focus.
Smart company	Innovation, subject specialization (either creative or analytical), knowledge management.
Portfolio owner	Financial acumen, good risk management skills.

Relationship management – the missing skill

There is one specific skill that will be needed in *all* the atoms that is likely to be in very short supply – relationship management.

In the mid-eighties, 5 percent of all revenue earned by Fortune 1000 companies was derived from alliances. By the end of the nineties, the figure had jumped to around 20 percent.[3] By the end of this decade (the noughties?) we expect that to be approaching 100 percent.

As we have seen, alliances offer a number of benefits over ownership – they are faster, (generally) don't require as much capital, they don't increase internal transaction costs and they represent an "option" to do future business rather than a firm commitment.

It's likely that the sketch of the atomized corporation that you produced in the last chapter included many atoms which are currently inside the corporate envelope, and some that would come from what are currently external sources.

Regardless of this mix, all of the atoms that you spin off or use will need to create, sustain, exploit and discard relationships both with the relics of the current corporation and with "external" players.

In a world where relationship capital is one of the major sources of intangible value, people who can manage these relationships will be at least as valuable as someone with superb operational skills.

Unfortunately, these relationship management skills are hard to find, and are often lacking in middle management in large corporations. This is not because the people are somehow deficient, but because they have been shielded from the need to develop them. Corporations that do not have a strong streak of entrepreneurship, that discourage or punish risk-taking, or that have a major "Not Invented Here" syndrome will have particular problems in this area.

Apart from having a clear strategic vision and the ability to find partners, the key skills in alliance management will be flexibility in the way that the relationship is managed, and that requires both forethought and formal processes governing the ways that exceptions and problems will be handled and the conditions under which the alliance will be dissolved.

PROTECT YOUR BRAND

The other area, alongside the development of relationship management skills, that atomizing corporations will have to carefully manage is that of creation and management of brand.

It is not easy to create a brand from scratch, but it is possible – think of how quickly Yahoo! and Amazon came to the fore. But most of the brands that will dominate the next decade will be the ones that have dominated the last two, and the ownership of these brands is a valuable source of wealth.

We talked in Chapter 6 of the importance of trust, and how that factor will be the element that dominates the consumer's perceptions and decisions. The grain around which the consumer's trust crystallizes is the brand that is attached to the offer. A promise broken is a brand damaged.

You may have read the works of other commentators on the new economy who say that the owners of the brand will become the centers of gravity around which consumers will flock, and that they will be the centers of gravity of the value web. Sorry, but we cannot agree with that. Companies like Shell and Ford, despite their many internal strengths and the universal recognition of their logos, simply do not have the degree of consumer understanding and intimacy that a customer manager atom will require.

Remember the example of Tesco and its banking partner that we used as a case study in Chapter 7? The brand attached to the offer was the one with which the customer would identify most, an example of brand-sharing and brand-loaning.

If you have a great brand but are production-centered (Shell, Ford), you can unlock the capital value inherent in the brand by brand-loaning. You'll remember the person in Chapter 8 who needed transport? The customer manager will create an offer for him that will include the strengths of multiple brands – think of the power of this offer: *"Yahoo! offers you a luxury car by Ford, financed by Citibank, and fuelled by Shell."*

Naturally, the brand-owning company will need to manage the brand aggressively to make sure that it is not diluted by poor delivery, by any component of the offer, to the end customer. And the one area that we would expect advertising and marketing to flourish is in the maintenance of brand awareness.

But which atom owns the brand of the dissolving company? There is no clear-cut formula that we can give to answer that question, other than "the one which is most sensible."

- For Shell's petrol products, the natural atom to own the brand will be the asset platform that does the refining.
- For Coca-Cola, which has little in the way of manufacturing of distribution of its own, we would expect a portfolio owner to manage and lease the brand as one of its assets.
- For a retail bank, which is trusted by its customers for its superb transaction processing skills despite indifferent customer intimacy, the logical way of maximizing the trust would be to locate the brand with the horizontal service platform.

VALUING THE ATOMS

Are the atoms viable?

If each of the atoms is to be run as a separate business, then it will need to survive on its own merits, competing against all other atoms of its type and against the unreconstructed corporations. It's time to draft a business plan for

SHELL

When Shell recently announced their desire to move from being an asset-based to a knowledge-based organization, they were expressing a desire to follow many of the principles expressed in this book. They were expressing the desire to unlock the value of their intangible assets, become smart, and play a more flexible role in their value web.

On hearing this you may think why on earth bother? The stock market judges them on the management of their oil revenues and physical assets, so why not focus on getting (even) better at this? By expressing this aim, what Shell are really saying is that they believe the real key to their value is not the management of their assets per se but the *knowledge* that enables them to do so. And that they want to explicitly unlock the value inherent in these capabilities.

For Shell, excelling at managing their assets means knowing how to extract full value from their oil sources in the shortest amount of time. This involves defining, holding and understanding a high degree of seismic information. It also involves a sophisticated set of partnering and relationship management skills; Shell's livelihood depends on their ability to maintain smooth relations with some of the most difficult governments in the world. And of course it involves a superlative host of program management skills. By seeking to explicitly focus on such capabilities, Shell are not only able to position themselves to benefit from an enhanced valuation based on new economy standards, but also to redefine their position in their value web. A skills portfolio such as this does not restrict you to drilling for oil or, for that matter, operating only in the oil industry. There would be nothing to stop Shell exploiting their relationship brokering skills to become the outsourced negotiating arm of any company or even any industry.

each atom that assesses its viability and predicts its worth. It might even be worth writing the plan as if it were an appeal to a venture capitalist for MBO funding (as it might well be ...).

Atomic profitability

Let's start by considering the atom in relation to the financials of the existing business. What proportion of the income, cost base, profit, asset depreciation (tangible and intangible) and debt does it represent?

Adjustments will be needed. Unless you have a rigorous internal trading system, it's likely that the customer-focused units do not carry the full cost of the corporate overheads. Similarly, support units may have low, or zero, direct revenue that does not reflect their contribution to the business.

The resolution to this is through benchmarking. What would the customer-focused unit pay on the open market for this showroom or that service? Or what would the accounts payable department realize for each invoice if it were charging on a commercial basis? It's important to use *external* market rates here, even if they are an estimate.[4]

You'll also have to calculate off-balance sheet items. Asset value is reasonably easy to calculate, as most of the tangible and intangible assets will be vested into a few atoms, but the capital worth and profitability of the atoms is harder to calculate – we'll come to that in the next section. But by the time you get to the end of this exercise, you will have an idea whether or not the atoms are viable as individual entities. If they do not appear to be viable, don't despair – we may have a solution.

What are the atoms worth now?

In order to work out what atoms you should float off from the corporation you will need an idea of what return they will bring to your shareholders – how profitable they will be and what the likely market capitalization will bring.

Amidst the sound of polishing of crystal balls, this section will start by introducing two measures to describe these factors and then attempt to estimate them using a method divided into three parts:

1   Estimating the profitability and likely market capitalization *excluding* the value of any released relational capital.

2   Adding in the effect of released relational capital.

3   Looking at the effects on the economy overall, to put these valuations in context.

Definitions first:

- Since we are looking at this from the point of view of the shareholder, we will measure profitability using *dividend yield*, which is a measure of the profit per share that the company returns to its owners (i.e. gross dividend) divided by the share price. Investors concerned with regular, safe income would choose industries that tended to return high dividend yields.

- We will get to market capitalizations using the *price/earnings ratio*, which is usually described as the ratio of the share price to the per-share earnings, where earnings are calculated after taxes, depreciation, interest etc have been deducted.[5] Alternatively it can be measured as the total market capitalization of the company divided by its after-tax (etc.) profit. The P/E can also be looked at as how many years the investor would have to hold the shares to get his money back.

Since there is little or no relational capital element in the valuation of today's corporations, the first part of our method of calculating the average dividend yields and P/E ratios of our atoms is to identify companies that are similar to the atom types. To do that, we have used averages for baskets of today's industries which most closely match the atom type.[6]

For example, figures for asset platforms are based on FTSE industry indices for 154 companies in a dozen asset-intensive industries.[7] The average dividend yield for this sample was 3.9 percent and the average P/E ratio was 13. Looking at the variability[8] in the sample, we can say that two thirds of companies in this sample will yield a profit of between 2.2 percent and 5.6 percent and a market capitalization of between 10 and 16 times their earnings.

Similarly, the figures for the horizontal service platforms were based on the mean of ten industries,[9] giving an average dividend yield of 2.4 percent, (with two thirds falling between 1.5–3.3 percent) and an average P/E of 21. with a typical spread between 17–25.

The figures for portfolio owners[10] gave a dividend yield of 1.5 percent and an average P/E of 73. We cannot calculate likely ranges in quite the same way, but a spread of ± 20 percent should be reasonable.

The figures for smart companies[11] are based on a single existing industry, with an average dividend yield of 0.3 percent and P/E of 108. As we have said previously, profitability and valuation of smart companies will be very volatile, so we think that these figures are likely to vary between 0 and 140 percent of these averages.

Customer managers and webspinners have yet to emerge in the shape that we envisage them, and we have not been able to use this method to estimate the value of the companies. But the basis of management consultancy is informed guesswork, and the figures in the table below are based on discussions with our colleagues.

The figures for the various types of atoms, excluding the relational capital element, are shown in Table 10.2.

Table 10.2 Profitability and P/E ratios excluding relational capital.

Atom	Average Div. Yield (%)	Two thirds between	Average P/E ratio	Two thirds between	Volatility
Asset platform	3.9%	2.2%–5.6%	13	10–16	Low
Service platform	2.4%	1.5%–3.3%	21	17–25	Low
Webspinner	~2%	1.5%–2.5%	30	20–50	Medium
Customer manager	2.5%	1.5%–3.5%	35	25–50	High
Smart company	0.3%	0.0%–0.4%	108	0–150	High
Portfolio owner	1.5%	1.2%–1.8%	73	58–87	Medium

We are the first to admit that this is an empirical method for calculating market caps and profits, but given the manifold uncertainties surrounding equities markets, the errors inherent in it are probably acceptable.

What we have not done yet is add in the relational capital element. And this is worth a considerable amount, as inspection of the new industrial giants such as Cisco and Enron (see case study, p. 101) show.

Figure 10.1 shows the relative proportions of physical, intellectual and relational capital that we think will exist in the atoms, once fully-formed and successful. Since this relational capital element does not exist in the corpora-

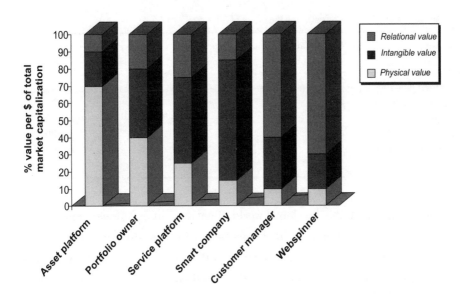

Figure 10.1 Proportions of physical, intangible and relational capital by atom type.

tions the atoms come from, we can treat this as additional wealth and calculate the uplift in P/E that atomization will cause – see Fig. 10.2 and Table 10.3.

Now for the context check. Does all of this make sense economically? As external transaction costs drop, much of the inefficiency in supply chains will be forced out. Competition will therefore force prices to drop, bringing an

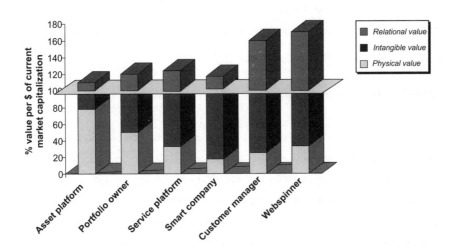

Figure 10.2 Relational capital expressed as new value.

Table 10.3 P/E ratios including the effect of relational capital.

Atom	Relational capital as % of total worth	Average P/E ratio now	Average P/E ratio once fully formed	Likely range
Asset platform	10	13	14	11–18
Service platform	25	21	28	23–33
Webspinner	70	30	100	60–150
Customer manager	60	35	60	40–80
Smart company	15	108	130	0–200
Portfolio owner	20	73	90	70–110

end to inflation in the developed world, if not a slight deflationary effect. Low interest rates will therefore drive more money into the stock markets, further strengthening the market capitalization of the atoms. So we think the figures are, if anything, underestimates and that that there will be a gradual but worthwhile increase in both average profitability and market capitalization of atoms as the next two decades proceed and the economy stabilizes around the new model. To put it another way, if a high proportion of mergers destroy shareholder capital, then it is likely that a high proportion of demergers will create new capital!

It should come as no surprise to anyone in an operational unit that the corporate center makes things worse. Indeed, Sadtler, Campbell and Koch[12] have estimated that the existence of a central control function in a corporation depresses its value by 10–50 percent, because of a number of factors including cost addition, demotivation, misinformation and (accidental) mismanagement.

Building the business plan

It's time to finish the business plan – to calculate the initial market capitalization of your atom, work out its likely annual profit after tax, depreciation, interest etc. and then multiply it by a P/E ratio from the appropriate range above – which end of the range your atom is at depends on its intellectual property and how strong its relationships are. Of course, you can't work out interest, depreciation etc. until you have a more or less full balance sheet for the atom, which is why we introduced the calculation of market capitalization last.

At the end of this process you should be able to put together a mini business plan that will give you a feeling for whether or not the atom is financially viable and whether its creation will be worthwhile.

Assuming the atom is viable, then ask yourself if it is good enough and cohesive enough to be able to win considerable external business now? If so, then why not let it start readying itself to trade in its own right before separation?

If the business is not viable, then two routes lie open to you. Many an atom will be too small, or only represent part of the services that would be needed for it to succeed, and here you should look for a business partner (perhaps a current competitor?) who has an atom with a complementary set of skills – we will talk more about collaborative atom creation in Chapter 12.

However, if the atom is already large enough, but you think it is too costly or just too lousy to survive, then you should plan to close the atom as soon as you can, and buy in those assets or services from outside – if it's not viable externally then it is not doing you any favors at the moment anyway!

SUMMARY

There is going to be some redundancy in your existing corporation and it will doubtless be a challenge for you to strip it out. You may also find that you are lacking some of the skill sets that will be needed to get the most out of the new atoms. Chief among these will probably be the most important skill of all – relationship management.

But these are short-term obstacles en route to a worthy long-term goal. We have explained how atomization releases previously trapped value. The handful of companies that are already some way down this road should be ample enough example of the sort of value we are talking about. Cisco and Enron, for example, have convincingly demonstrated relational worth to the stock market and been applauded in return.

There will be skeptics, but if we are right about the associated explosion of relational capital unleashed by atomization then shareholders have every reason to be optimistic in the years ahead.

CHAPTER 11

Industrial (R)evolution

INTRODUCTION

W E HAVE LOOKED AT the atomization process at the level of the corporation. Now it is time to look at what it will mean for entire industries.
We expect it to sweep across the entire economic panoply, leaving no corner
untouched. This chapter will outline some of the opportunities in the biggest
sectors and build on where the process has already begun to manifest itself.

We will deal with financial services, the energy sector, telecommunications, consumer products, and information technology, pausing in each to discuss where our atoms fit into the way the sector works at present and will work
in the future.

As with re-engineering in the nineties we expect to see a progressive
atomization sweep across different industrial sectors, having started already
in the areas of consumer products and IT, and moving rapidly into telecommunications and financial services (Fig. 11.1).

WHICH ATOMIZATION STRATEGIES TO PURSUE?

We have already introduced a framework to describe the atomization possibilities, based on separation of competency from focus (see Chapter 7). Remember
the three main strategic options:

- *Excellence* – leveraging scale and scope to build cost advantage and leadership. This implies focus on asset and service platforms that operate across,
  and beyond, entire sectors.
- *Innovation* – creating agile, knowledge-intensive design shops (smart
  companies) that can innovate product or service to respond to changing

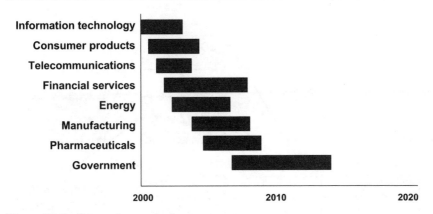

Figure 11.1 Progressive atomization across sectors.

customer needs. An example of this includes BMW's US-based design house, Innovation Associates.

■ *Intimacy* – building close relationships with customers to anticipate and respond to individual needs. Data mining skills and interactive channels are core competencies here. Cendent set its ambitions in this direction with Avis and other service-based acquisitions. We see separation of consumers and business customers reflected in our two types of atom, customer managers and webspinners.

The diversity of focus and skills required almost prevents companies from excelling across all three areas, and they must thus concentrate on one activity that reflects most closely their strategic intent and core competencies. For example, American Express has adopted operational excellence as its mantra in a sector of constantly changing financial products.

In our atomized economy, we expect to see major corporations divesting all but the core atoms that align directly with their strategic intent, yet holding equity positions elsewhere to secure value in the broader economic ecosystem in which they operate. For example, The Coca-Cola Company (TCCC) has already divested much of its manufacturing and distribution activities to independent bottlers and distributors, choosing to retain only "smart company" activities such as brand and product formulation management. But it continues to hold equity in these other entities (Fig. 11.2).

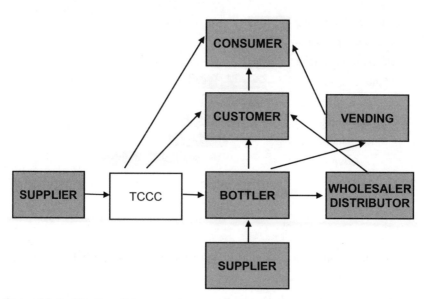

Figure 11.2 The Coca-Cola ecosystem.

In the sections below we examine the forces at work in key industry sectors and consider the likely routes for atomization of the principal players into our six atom types. We also summarize the strategic choices available to market leaders by applying the above framework.

RETAIL BANKING AND INSURANCE

Companies in the retail financial services sector focus exclusively on consumers and small businesses, providing finance and cash-based transaction services. In addition to maintaining major transaction-based IT platforms, they service customers through a proliferating number of channels to market (call centers, branches, Internet, interactive TV etc.). Some more adventurous players have leveraged their extensive cross-sector customer base by expanding into horizontal marketplaces.[1]

These industries are consolidating rapidly because they need to achieve both a broad spread of product and associated economies of scale in transaction processing and market channel coverage. Customer loyalty is reasonably strong (albeit for basic services), and trust (brand) is vitally important.

The atomization opportunity is immense in this sector. We expect to see:

- *Customer managers (the financial services retailer)* – atoms able to anticipate customer needs on a one-to-one basis and build a strong emotional
offer, for example, "financial security for life." Brand will be an important
asset to these atoms, as will access to appropriate market channels. We
expect to see aggressive involvement from outside the traditional banking
sector, for example from companies like Wal-Mart, Tesco and Carrefour.

- *Webspinners (service integrators)* – atoms able to bundle together a broad
range of financial and related services to deliver attractive offers to consumers and small businesses. These may well combine financial and non-
financial products as finance is integrated more closely into other offers, for
example, property and vehicle ownership. We expect to see a growing emphasis on horizontal markets providing financial support services to small
businesses and high net worth individuals.

- *Smart companies (product innovators)* – atoms specializing in the creation
and rapid launch of innovative financial products and services. Specialist
units such as actuarial services will become part of interesting new cross-
sector alliances (e.g. telecommunications and consumer products) pooling
brand and technology know-how with financial products.

- *Service platforms* – the most obvious role for this sector lies in the creation of
low-cost transaction platforms to handle cash transactions and services such
as claims processing. Leading banks and insurance groups will co-invest in
these platforms, probably hand-in-hand with IT service companies.

- *Asset platforms* – large banks, in particular, have a significant asset base,
ranging from High Street branch properties to shared call centers and Internet portals. It is likely that new atoms will emerge to leverage this, again
with co-investment from beyond the sector (e.g. retailing, IT services).

- *Portfolio owners* – if there is one thing that retail banks and insurance
companies have, it is a lot of their customer's cash. We would expect
that these organizations will be counted amongst the new portfolio owners
holding, as assets, a range of atoms (their own and others) and a variety of
business assets (e.g. insurance risks), often integrated by a strong brand
umbrella.

So we see a clear segregation emerging between the ownership of the customer, the processing of the transactions, and exploitation of the cash held. While many of the retail banks would regard themselves as customer facing, we suspect that their knowledge of their mass market customers is patchy at best, and they may struggle to survive on their own as customer managers.

The options for major banks and insurance companies are clear. They should detach their costly and cumbersome branch networks from their back-office operations. There are great opportunities for collaborative ventures, either in product innovation and customer relationship management with the help of others, or in superbly efficient transaction processing.

The implications for structural changes are as follows. Leading financial institutions will become holding, or "portfolio" companies with interests ranging across all the above atoms, integrated by a strong brand umbrella. Some will choose to focus on smart company atoms to achieve product and service excellence, but share equity in customer managers, webspinners and asset/service platforms. Others will focus on retailing aspects and building high customer intimacy.

The separation between manufacturer and customer manager (retailer) will become ever more apparent as atomization accelerates across the sector.

WHOLESALE AND CORPORATE BANKING

In this sector, global consolidation is being driven by the need to realize scale and scope advantages as well as global customer coverage. Corporate banking has been, and will always remain, relationship driven, with highly paid and knowledgeable staff manning the front line to the customer. Financial products are bundled currently with high quality research because this is necessary to sustain customer interest and loyalty. Large commercial transactions, such as underwriting new flotations, involve high elements of risk, with syndication a key competency.

Market-making is another core competency, with liquidity a prime driver in recent consolidations amongst global players. Dealing operations themselves have been consolidated into regional centers with a wide range of instruments being traded.

Some banks have chosen to play in horizontal e-service markets to extend their presence into client back offices, for example, by offering cash management. The client networks of many banks – spanning every sector – are a major relational asset waiting to be exploited

Atomization opportunities are large, although leading players remain keen to retain strategic control over a wide range of activities. Some opportunities include:

- *Customer (or relationship) managers* – the core skill of many corporate banks will remain focused on relationships and could spawn a range of consulting and research services alongside traditional transactional capabilities. Goldman Sachs neatly fits into this category – perhaps it should consider acquiring McKinsey?

- *Webspinners (or syndication specialists)* – syndication of multiple institutions around major transactions could migrate to specialized atoms that have wide network connections and can manage risk effectively. The personal networks and relationships of key staff will be of great advantage here as well as corporate brand.

- *Smart companies (thought leadership)* – the high quality research undertaken by institutions to support clients could offer a lucrative new source of revenue and equity value, and we think it will migrate to new atoms able to leverage the intellectual property more widely. Consequently, we expect to see more spin-offs of primary research activities to rival traditional consultancies such as Gartner and Forrester.

- *Service platforms (transaction processing)* – many of the back-office operations of banks could be amalgamated into sector-wide platforms. The infrastructures supporting dealing operations and client channels may also become candidates for new service platforms. Watch out for shared dealing rooms – hotel style.

- *Service platforms (market transaction engines)* – the consolidation of financial trading markets is set to accelerate now that US markets such as NAS-DAQ have come knocking on European doors. These consolidations will present opportunities for global service platforms handling transactions on a huge scale. We expect some dramatic developments here as major players pool their trading assets to expand liquidity and lower transaction costs.

■ *Portfolio owners* – we foresee the operation of markets[2] changing radically with the current market-makers becoming, in effect, portfolio owners in collaboration with the venture capitalists and mutual fund managers. As we identified in the previous bullet point, the markets themselves may lose their physical presence entirely, becoming virtual horizontal service platforms ensuring settlement and providing assurance and identification services.

With the predictable divestment and merging of back-office infrastructures and trading platforms, financial institutions and marketplaces will be left to concentrate on developing smaller, high value Atomic Corporations that excel in one of the following areas:

■ managing large and complex corporate relationships (customer managers);

■ generating quality research and data to lubricate the world's customer channels and trading marketplaces (smart companies); and

■ offering powerful syndication capabilities with appropriate risk management controls (webspinners).

The fragmentation of the overall financial services sector is shown in Fig. 11.3.

ENERGY SECTOR (OIL AND GAS)

Private investors regard most companies in the energy sector as defensive stocks, with relatively low P/E ratios but exceptional profits. One or two exceptions exist – Enron focuses on market-making activities and is highly rated by the stock market. However, much of the world's energy assets remain in government hands and are likely to continue to do so despite privatization pres-

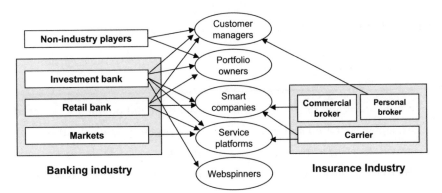

Figure 11.3 Atomization of the banking industry.

sures. Industry consolidation has taken place in recent years, especially in the oil and gas sector where the industry remains highly fragmented – Exxon Mobil is the market leader but only has a six percent market share of global oil revenues. Regular and often unpredictable fluctuations in the price of crude oil leads to high volatility in profits, as well as political and social sensitivities.

In the oil sector, the majority of profit is derived from upstream activities – exploration and production – where quality of asset management determines stock market valuations. To offset the high cost of these capitally-intensive and speculative activities, much of the infrastructure is shared amongst the major players, for example, in the North Sea and Alaska.

The oil majors have historically favored vertical integration, linking well head to petrol pump, with Exxon Mobil, Chevron-Texaco, Shell, BP etc. being the principal petrochemical retailers across the world. This has been motivated by the need to guarantee market access for highly profitable exploration and production activities.

Although this vertical integration means that many of the oil majors are global retailers with tens of thousands of outlets (including convenience stores), institutions have difficulty valuing this activity alongside upstream assets. Skeptics would argue that downstream operations add little to overall shareholder value, indicating a strong atomization opportunity.

Upstream atomization

Atomization is already apparent in upstream:

■ *Shared asset and service platforms* – exploration and production are good examples of how oil and gas companies have worked together with service providers to share investment and spread risk.

■ *Smart companies* – a few knowledge-rich companies with expertise in seismic data extraction and analysis serve the energy majors. Others specialize in process innovation such as well drilling and crude extraction.

We expect further atomization in upstream activities as some majors choose to become portfolio owners of exploration assets, and migrate away from operational responsibilities and associated physical assets. Shell has already declared its intention to become a knowledge-based company rather than a physical, asset-based concern.

Downstream atomization

In downstream – from the refineries to the petrol pump – new atomization opportunities exist, driven by the pressures to increase operating efficiencies and better leverage customer relationships:

■ *Customer managers (energy service retailers)* – retailing of petroleum and gas products is a commodity business with low customer loyalty and high government taxation. Although petroleum retailers know very little about the majority of their customers, an opportunity exists to bring wider on-land retail and on-line customer relationship skills to this area, requiring some radical thinking and possibly joint ventures with companies outside the sector such as Nokia or Coca-Cola.

■ *Webspinners (energy market makers)* – relationships with corporate customers are often good and could well be broadened to meet a growing range of energy-focused needs. Oil companies are under pressure to expand the scope of their current offerings to escape commodity traps, and corporations such as Enron have taken a lead position here (as shown in Chapter 7). Already, market-making atoms such as LevelSeas[3] and OceanConnect[4] have been established by the major players.

■ *Smart companies (knowledge based)* – operations such as refining require intensive sector knowledge, reflecting the complex processes surrounding energy extraction, production and distribution (see the ShipChem study below). Many of the oil majors have resident expertise that could be spun off into smart companies focusing on product and process innovation.

■ *Asset platforms (global refining systems)* – by far the most exciting opportunity is to aggregate downstream assets such as refineries, pipelines and storage depots into a sector-wide asset platform serving the whole industry. And we expect further activity motivated by an economic need to better optimize regional and global capacity.

SHIPCHEM

There is also scope to utilize industry-specific assets to create Service platforms. Eastman Chemical effectively outsourced its logistics arm (which handled the specialized carriage of oil and chemicals) to a new venture, ShipChem, in March 2000. ShipChem is a joint venture with a supplier of logistics and transportation software, G-Log.

It is based on the backbone of the Eastman logistics network, but it relies on the Internet to gather its customers and co-ordinate its network of partners, providing optimization, management, tracking and payment management for specialist multimodal shipping.

Energy companies have an inbred managerial culture linked closely to their upstream exploration activities. Long-term success in the oil sector frequently relates to exploration rather than production and distribution, that is, picking the best exploration sites. Retailing activities lie far from these core competencies and are candidates for divestment.

So we would expect energy companies to atomize (see Fig. 11.4) by adopting one or more of the following strategies:

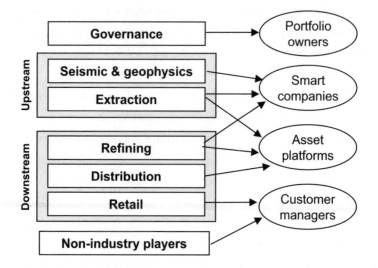

Figure 11.4 Atomization of the oil and gas industry.

- apply *smart company* thinking in the complex and risky area of exploration of energy sources (oil, gas and renewable) and in the management of their major assets (refining and exploration);
- focus on *customer management* in collaboration with other sectors (for example, consumer products or business services);
- possibly offload forecourt operations and convenience stores onto the retail sector;
- offload much of the asset-intensive downstream activity such as refining and distribution to global *asset platforms* supporting all players in the sector – but retaining an equity holding; and
- create trading markets, or *webspinners*, between key operators within the sector to increase efficiency and decrease volatility of supply.

TELECOMMUNICATIONS OPERATORS

As we have already discussed, the telecoms sector requires huge investment. The leading companies in the industry spend about 20 percent of sales on capital investment and it is no surprise that many of them are laden with debt. Competition is strong from a number of sources (cable, wireless and satellite), a glut of bandwidth means that current services are commoditizing rapidly, and new services are clouded in uncertainty.[5] Correspondingly, stock market valuations and credit ratings for telcos have slipped dramatically in recent times, increasing the cost of capital for much needed investments.

National telecom operators continue to be vertically integrated, owning both core network assets and the channels to customer (including local connection, billing, and customer support services). Many telcos, such as BT, have expanded across regions through a patchwork of joint ventures and cross-equity holdings.

Break-up is the public intent of many of the larger operators such as AT&T, BT and MCI-Worldcom, but progress has been slow and investors are becoming impatient. Likely moves here include spin-offs of component parts such as wireless activities, local distribution networks and joint ventures.

Our atomization model could take this thinking a lot further and corresponds to recent models from research companies such as Mainspring (Table 11.1). Applying our framework, we envisage the following possibilities:

■ *Customer managers (telecom service retailers)* – atoms that own the consumer relationship could become highly valued companies given the growing impact of telecommunications on our lives and the linkage to lifestyles. However, new mechanisms for unlocking value are needed, with pricing based on application rather than simple usage (line/minutes). In the commercial sector we expect to see more niche players serving specialist corporate/sector needs and maximizing relationship value.

■ *Smart companies (new service incubators)* – atoms that focus on product and service innovation, especially in new areas such as 3G. These companies could provide incubation facilities for players emerging from other sectors (e.g. automotive, media, consumer goods, banking), which are all interested in exploiting new interactive channels to the customer. Expect network equipment providers to jump in here.

■ *Asset platforms (shared networks)* – the glut of bandwidth and high levels of investment needed to construct new networks implies a strong case for industry-wide consolidation towards a small number of global and local network operators. These could be co-owned by major telecom operators,

Table 11.1 – Mainspring's view of atomization in the telecoms sector.

Mainspring's name	Mainspring's description	Correspondence to atom type
CompleteCo	Offers a complete portfolio of communications services, which it markets and sells to end users and other communications companies.	In our terms, a webspinner capable of buying and selling unused capacity. Several "bandwidth exchanges" are emerging to fill this role.
LongHaul	Owns a global high-capacity communications infrastructure.	A global asset platform, probably formed from the merger of assets floated from several local providers.
NetCo	Owns the physical infrastructure to provide transport for any communications needs and networking services.	Asset platform, owning and operating networks at a regional and local level.
WirelessCo	Owns, operates local wireless services and markets to end users.	Asset platform.
BillCo	Owns systems and infrastructure to perform billing functions for communications service providers.	Service platform, probably working at a national level. There may be potential to provide billing services for far more than just communications.
MarketCo	Markets and provides access to a broad variety of communications services to end users.	A mix of webspinners and customer managers, depending on the target market.

reflecting the fact that bandwidth provision is no longer a sustainable competitive advantage. Cable & Wireless is pursuing just such a strategy.

■ *Webspinners (market-makers)* – strong opportunities exist to trade excess bandwidth capacity, as we have seen in the case of Enron and Duke Energy. A range of secondary instruments is likely to emerge based on variable demand patterns. We expect to see financial institutions climb on board here!

■ *Service platforms (intelligent billing)* – areas such as billing and maintenance offer attractive opportunities for service platform providers, especially if the opportunity to bill for services other than telecoms are included. Specialist knowledge is needed and investment in new tools is high, and we would expect service platforms to be created in collaboration with IT service companies.

With the inevitable move towards break-up and atomization, leading telecom operators will retain a portfolio management role, spreading shareholder interests across current commodity services (the cash generators) and innovative new ones (high risk). The market will continue to regard traditional voice and data services (even Internet) as utility businesses, thus downgrading stock valuations for companies concentrating in this area.

But separation out of network platform activities should improve analyst ratings, and leave these companies to focus on customer relationships. Much higher valuations will go to smart companies and webspinners operating in the new service area – where service creation and risk management processes are regarded as core competencies. Watch out for more companies like Enron.

CONSUMER PRODUCTS

As with the oil sector, many of the leading consumer products companies are seen as defensive stocks with low historic revenue growth and mature products. Also of concern to investors is the likely impact of electronic markets on supply relationships with their principal customers – the retailers. In a world that is becoming increasingly interactive, questions have also been raised about whether toothpaste and soap powders can be made into sexy brands. The move towards global economies of scale, accelerated by business re-engineering in the nineties, has burdened these companies with large-scale manufacturing units and complex processes, deeply embedded in electronic concrete (often referred to as ERP systems).

This sector took early advantage of vertical marketplaces. Transora was established by no fewer than 63 sponsor companies ranging from Coca-Cola to Proctor & Gamble. Many companies have also experimented with consumer portals to achieve closer links with end customers, although many fear a backlash from retailers.

As discussed earlier in this chapter, one company in this sector has escaped low stock ratings by atomizing early in its existence – Coca-Cola. It has achieved outstanding market capitalization, with consistently high P/E ratios. Coca-Cola is a twenty-billion-dollar company operating in a two-hundred-billion-dollar system, focusing exclusively on brand development and product formulation, and outsourcing the bulk of manufacture and distribution to bottlers and others in the supply chain. It retains cross-share holdings in its main business partners to leverage value from the entire system.

The case for atomization in this sector has never been higher, with stock values falling by up to 50 percent in recent times. Mechanisms to unlock value include:

■ *Customer manager (lifestyle portals)* – new atoms focused on consumer lifestyle, building Internet-based portals that could generate new sources of equity value from established brands. The recent launch by Proctor & Gamble of Reflect.com, a health and beauty portal, is a good example, leveraging established brand equity.

■ *Smart companies (design shops)* – atoms that focus on product innovation and employ highly skilled designers and technologists will command high equity values. The concept of an innovation factory that accelerates new product development is being explored by a number of leading players.

■ *Asset and service platforms (divestment)* – consumer product companies employ vast infrastructures that add little value to the core business. Many have chosen to outsource IT and accounting, but have benefited little from these moves in equity terms. Transora is an industry experiment that could be the forerunner to many more co-operative schemes, ranging from shared financial services to employee portals. The latter would be held as either private or quoted stock, thus retaining value amongst key customers.

The Coca-Cola model of an atomized company has much to recommend it. The core value is locked in the brand – it can be leveraged through *customer management* atoms, and in the product formulation embedded in *smart com-*

pany atoms. Both have high value profiles. The rest of the infrastructure, from factories and distribution to processes and systems, could be divested into jointly held asset platforms that return equity value to their primary customers.

INFORMATION TECHNOLOGY

Being the primary growth engine of the new economy, this sector has become increasingly complex and diverse. It spans hardware and software, as well as IT services such as consulting and systems integration. Leading companies in the sector such as Microsoft, Oracle and IBM are frequently first to apply new techniques to improve the performance of their own businesses, and some IT corporations like Cisco have adopted atomization ideas ahead of the crowd (in Cisco's case by divesting generic processes such as production in favor of higher value design and customer service activities – thus becoming a smart company).

Technology itself has had, and will continue to have, a transformational effect on the structure of the sector. Most recently, it has stimulated new manufacturing models in PC suppliers such as Dell, Compaq and Gateway, based on zero inventory and personalized production. The Internet has had an equally profound effect on the sector with the development of new e-business and e-service offerings. New players such as Commerce One and Ariba are now vying for position against traditional competitors.

The IT sector has always taken full advantage of its innovative business practices to enhance customer relationships across all areas of commerce and government. For example, new consulting firms such as Index and Gemini brought re-engineering to their clients in the eighties, and their parents, CSC and CAP, created new ERP and system integration opportunities in the nineties. The recent entry of the "fast five" agencies such as Viant, Scient and Sapient is helping many traditional organizations to introduce Web-based processes and customer portals.

Atomization has already taken root in this sector with the growing separation of information and knowledge-based processes and asset-based operations.

We anticipate further atomization of the major players into the following components:

- *Customer managers (account-focused service organizations)*: similar to investment banks, many IT service organizations have invested heavily in building strong customer relationships on a global and regional basis. These help to elevate the role of technology on the corporate agenda and stimulate higher value service opportunities.

- *Smart company (product innovators):* most of the big breakthroughs in IT come from small, venture-backed technology companies. These companies exploit the raft of consultancies and system integrators to bring product to market. Many are acquired by global leaders such as Cisco, Microsoft and IBM once the product has proved itself in the markets.

- *Webspinners (system integrators):* complex customer needs require a myriad of IT products and services. These in turn have led to a network of alliances and partnerships across the sector. Many large IT service firms have three hundred or more such alliances. Developing and managing these alliances demands specific skills and is a potential source of revenue.

- *Asset and service platforms:* companies such as EDS and Cap Gemini Ernst & Young are good at operating IT platforms on behalf of their clients. In addition, IT companies such as Hewlett-Packard have recognized the need to divest many of their generic processes to simplify their businesses and to cut cost. They recognize that such services could become a significant component to future income if shared with other partners or clients. Many new developments are expected in this area, as we shall see in the next chapter.

So some commodity IT product and service providers may evolve towards a virtual company with a single point of contact for customers, employees, suppliers and other stakeholders. This could be a combination of customer manager and webspinner. Meanwhile, much of the product and service innovation will be undertaken by venture-backed smart companies who may forge special relationships with the other players.

HEWLETT-PACKARD

Under the direction of CEO Carleton Fiorina, Hewlett-Packard is in the business of transforming itself from a steady hardware giant into a strategic e-services and Internet player.

From its roots in a Palo Alto garage in 1938 when it was set up by engineers Bill Hewlett and David Packard, HP's strengths have been in the manufacturing of reliable hardware systems: ink-jet printers, Unix servers and workstations, storage devices and back-up systems. More than 80 percent of sales come from computing and print operations, with IT services accounting for only 15 percent. Presaged partly by recent missed sales targets and slowed growth of the core business, and partly by the fact that hardware will continue to be commoditized at ever higher performance levels, HP are aiming for a strategic shift towards growth oriented e-services and software.

What the world needs, according to HP, is an "always on infrastructure that delivers e-services to a bevy of mobile applications" and they are building software and services capability in line to support this. Recognizing that e-business is more about improving relationships with clients, suppliers, and employees through the Web than it is about product loyalty, HP are looking to broaden their services into the areas of application hosting, on-line brokering, Web-based learning, and support for mobile devices.

Undeterred by the failure to acquire the IT consulting arm of PriceWaterhouseCoopers, HP are looking to build consulting skills in-house. They claim to have added 1700 consultants in 2001, and aim to add another 1500 in the near future. While HP appears to be going in the opposite direction to our atomization trend, we predict that, once the components are in place, they will spawn a host of smaller buinesses.

For those IT companies focusing on providing a full range of services to large corporate clients, the core strategic direction will again fall within customer manager and webspinner. However, we expect these companies to take an increasingly active part in spawning atoms to operate shared services on behalf of their main customers.

SUMMARY

The path is now wide open for atomization across all major commercial sectors, but the main incumbents will need to choose the roles they want to take. Enron, Cisco, and Coca-Cola are all market-leaders in their respective sectors and are well prepared for the demands of the new economy. They have focused on their core competence and structured their existing business to make the most of their longstanding relationships. The markets have accordingly rated them highly.

Examples of atomization strategies will be:

- *Customer manager* – favored by both retail organizations and business-to-business companies that are prepared to invest heavily in becoming the partner of choice to selected major accounts (such as investment banking and IT Services). Consumer management (such as financial and energy retailing) is a potential gold mine, but one where the incumbents have a long way to go before they become intimate with their customers.
- *Webspinners* are of central importance in the delivery of lifestyle offers to consumers. Players here will search for and bundle together different products and services to meet an individual customer need. They are also important in business services such as IT and investment banking where integration of offers is complex and risky.
- *Smart companies* – this is an attractive niche where exceptional human talent and venture funds can create new product and service innovations, as well as process improvements. The agility and creativity of such organizations merits separation from traditional economy players. But these firms will need to exploit the scope and scale of global asset platforms to produce the necessary economic returns for shareholders and employees.
- *Asset* and *service platform* creation is an unstoppable movement, producing global platforms that operate on behalf of a small number of major players. These platforms will extend the current models of shared services into e-services, applicable to every generic business process – from both front and back office.

The Global 2000 companies of the future will choose to excel in one of the above areas, whilst holding equity positions in other atoms. By so doing they will be able to retain and enhance value inherent in their current organizational structures whilst simplifying their operations down to a single core competence.

Atomization is going to radically change most industrial sectors. They will each have their different demands and will evolve in subtly different directions. But the common theme will be a reorientation around the newly empowered customer. There are clues to the future in some sectors, where outstanding corporations have already begun the process of atomization or been organized along sympathetic lines for some time.

CHAPTER 12

New Partnerships, New Wealth

INTRODUCTION

W E HAVE TOLD YOU what to look for in your corporation, suggested what you might want to do with what you find, and predicted how it will affect the industries that you work in. But we haven't yet talked about how to manage that change.

We would suggest that atomization will require an even more intense management effort, with a significant part played at the very highest level. And it will eventually go beyond the corporations' own shores. Collaboration, already a vital part of the connected economy, will be moved even more to the center of the stage. Relational capital, after all, is the most important value unlocked by the process of atomization.

HARNESSING CORPORATE E-INITIATIVES

The combination of e-business and the connected economy has been the most challenging wave to wash over corporate shores since the introduction of the computer itself some forty years ago. Many firms have committed their most senior executives to orchestrate fundamental changes. Well-publicized examples are BP's launch of their Digital Business division, headed by their erstwhile CIO, and the appointment of the deputy chairman of Chase as their e-business supremo.

These same corporations have launched ambitious internal change programs to exploit Web-based processes and structures, dramatically increasing corporate speed and agility through widespread e-working. These initiatives will make the corporation work better and will partially stabilize its structure by reducing internal transaction costs. And they should be encouraged, even if they may be overtaken by events.

The early years of the new millennium saw enormous overreaction in favor of, and later against, consumer-focused dot.com businesses. We have also seen a torrent of announcements around the formation of vertical market-places, as we discussed in Chapter 8. Cap Gemini Ernst & Young's view on the rise and fall of the e-marketplace can be seen in Fig. 12.1.

The majority of the Global 2000 corporations are now committed to play-ing in at least one vertical e-marketplace and several horizontal markets. You know how we feel about these – those that are well executed and which have a proposition based on long-term value will transform their industry and bring tremendous wealth to their owners. The rest, and that means most of them, will fail.

So what are the approaches taken so far to this wave of change, and how can corporations better prepare themselves for the atomized economy?

Working with several hundred major corporations around the world we have detected a repeated pattern of approach towards the connected economy, with corporations initiating three classes of e-business project:

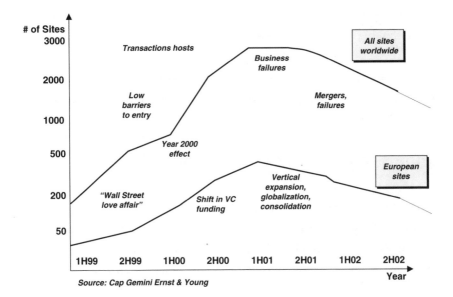

Source: Cap Gemini Ernst & Young

Figure 12.1   E-marketplace consolidation.

- *Protect the core*: projects in this category invariably address internal process improvement by applying Web-based technologies to critical work activities such as product development, order fulfillment and customer service. The outcome is a stronger business, able to sustain increasingly competitive environments.

- *Change the game*: new Web-based techniques can be used here to extend the current business model into new products and services. For example, on-line customer portals based on established business relationships can offer a combination of existing and new services, the latter derived from external business partners. An oil retailer may introduce Internet connections to its garage forecourts to build a broader on-line relationship with its many customers.

- *Create the new*: here, connected solutions may open up entirely new ways of doing business in a particular sector such as consumer products, often with radical new solutions. An established player may choose to exploit its competencies to open up new "white space" business opportunities aligned with its broader business mission – that is, those that are not already addressed by existing business units. For example, Proctor & Gamble launched Reflect.com to become the world's leading health and beauty portal – away from its traditional coverage of toothpaste and hair care, but continuing to exploit consumer relationships.

The consensus on investment priority suggests a split of resources as shown in Fig. 12.2, although it varies as corporations' use of e-business becomes more mature.

ADOPTING NEW GOVERNANCE MODELS

Following a wave of high-level corporate appointments and new e-projects, the dust is beginning to settle. Many of the early players recognize that frenetic activity alone will not produce the desired results. Alignment of business need and Web technology investment continues to work its way up to the top of leading management issues – hot on the heels of corporate IT spend.

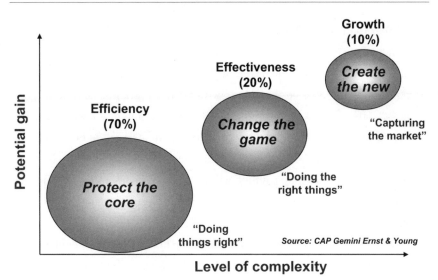

Figure 12.2   Protect the core, change the game, create the new.

We think that a focus on e-business will prove to be a short-lived phenomenon that will rapidly be reabsorbed into the mainstream of business strategy and management. In two years time we do not expect to hear the dreaded "e" being spoken. It will be business as usual.

But the pace of atomization is unlikely to abate. Shareholder pressure will see to that. Major corporations will continue to seek new ways of divesting non-core assets such as HR and finance, whilst focusing on activities higher up the value chain, such as knowledge-based divisions associated with product innovation and customer management.

The corporations will need enlightened and powerful management committees able to comprehend both the opportunities and appropriate mechanisms for atom creation. We anticipate atomization planning and operational activities to be spread across all levels of major corporations – corporate center, business division and business operating unit.

■ *At the corporate level*: strategic debate will focus on future corporate structures and core competencies across the group. Issues of which corporate services to consolidate and divest will resemble earlier debates on corporate break-up. The main concern will be to optimize shareholder value by releasing potential energy associated with the complex corporate DNA.

Further interest will be to invest in "white space" possibilities that represent an opportunity to "create the new."

■ *At the divisional level*: managers will be more pragmatic, focusing on opportunities to "change the game" within their particular sphere of business – often by linking resources across two or more operating units. The atomized future will mean that opportunities to form value networks with corporations outside their direct area of competition will be high on the agenda. Divisional management will also take responsibility for prioritizing e-projects according to the classification described above – see Fig. 12.2.

■ *At the operating unit level*: the main attention here will be to protect the core of the business by Web-enabling the individual business processes and broader business infrastructure. This will both save money and increase the competitiveness and agility of the potential atoms. Opportunities to electronically network by participating in markets and infomediaries within the supply chain become attractive at this level. Extending the unit into wider communities of employees and customers becomes feasible with the availability of portals.

WHAT IS THE FUTURE ROLE OF
THE CORPORATE CENTER?

As e-business enters the mainstream, the role of the corporate center as the direct controller of operations should begin to diminish still further. As with any parenting activity, the onslaught of e-business merits an intensive but limited period of corporate intervention to ensure that business divisions and units exploit the new technologies and commercial opportunities. Seed funding and thought leadership are the main contributing factors of the center at this early stage of business adoption. Thereafter, the center is well advised to adopt a monitoring role to ensure that programs are executed and necessary resources deployed.

In the context of atomization, the corporate center will clearly migrate into the role of a portfolio owner, and will need to steer divisional and business unit initiatives to maximize perceived increases in shareholder value.

The recent commitment of Hewlett-Packard's CEO to divest a wide range of corporate services to reduce operating costs and develop strategic investments outside the corporation is illustrative of such an intervention. Similarly, Shell's plan to move towards becoming a knowledge-based organization will require a major restructuring of human and financial resources.

In summary, e-business presents a serious challenge to global corporations, especially in the context of atomization. The knee-jerk reaction to pull all e-initiatives into the corporate center may be appropriate in the early stages but rapidly loses touch with the realities and discrete needs of the individual business units.

MEETING THE EXPECTATION GAP

The increasingly radical nature of initiatives to unlock new forms of capital is bound to raise many doubts and uncertainties. Stresses are already apparent in vertical marketplaces where competing organizations try to co-operate. Some e-business initiatives already look doomed to fail despite their initial promise, and most executives will admit that returns from current e-business investments have been far from spectacular.

Many vertical market programs are trailing years behind initial forecasts, with the real prospect of alienating line management and shareholders alike. Likewise, internal projects to re-engineer key business processes using Web technologies have been met with all the organizational and cultural resistance of the re-engineering boom in the nineties. It has not been quite the dot.com blow-out witnessed in first quarter of 2000 but there have been all the classic signs of corporate inertia.

In short, there is a growing gap between expectations and outcomes. So how do we avoid the inevitable impasse?

Bold ideas are needed to overcome the inertia. We will now describe one of the most ambitious collaborative approaches to emerge in the new era, and outline the governance, or corporate parenting, necessary to create a rapid and sustained response to the connected economy.

BUILDING A NEW COLLABORATIVE APPROACH

One of the central planks of our thesis is that relational capital will become the main source of sustained value in the digital economy. And in a truly connected economy, no single organization can expect to retain a monopoly over relationships. Just as the spread of knowledge management was driven by the realization that knowledge is power only if it is shared rather than retained, so the relational capital boom will be driven by the realization that the value of a relationship is greatly enhanced by mutual trust.

To create the atoms and ensure their survival, tomorrow's leaders will need to work together rather more closely to generate collective rather than individual advantage.

Early on in the new millennium, Cap Gemini Ernst & Young, along with a handful of other global consultancy firms, helped to facilitate collective corporate ventures to prepare its clients for the atomized economy. In the context of the Atomic Corporation, the primary purpose of these ventures was to precipitate the formation of service platforms, housing one or more of the generic processes of the participating corporations – for example, finance and human resources.

By bringing together world-class corporations from across industry sectors with complementary skills, we discovered that such partnerships could:

- *accelerate internal transformation*: sharing of innovative e-business practices across sector boundaries has helped to compress adoption cycles and bring new thinking to traditional corporations; and
- *enhance external stakeholder perception*: by co-developing new venture vehicles that demonstrate global leadership in e-business transformation. These ventures generate separate market ratings and provide pathways to exciting new IPO offerings.

WHAT MIGHT THE INITIAL OFFERINGS BE?

The early collective experience of developing vertical procurement markets such as Trade Ranger (Energy) and Covisint (Automotive) has to an extent

THE INTERNET SERVICES VENTURE VEHICLE (ISVV)

Whilst the commercial world pursued the formation of vertical e-procurement markets in early 2000, a unique collaborative venture based on a service platform was being explored by twelve of the world's largest corporations. This venture was code named the ISVV and was sponsored by BP, CGEY and Hewlett-Packard. Early parties registering interest in the venture included such prestige names as Coca-Cola, Proctor & Gamble, Morgan Stanley Dean Witter and American Express.

The concept driving the ISVV was the possibility that beyond the early formation of vertical e-procurement markets would be a likely succession of other opportunities derived from global connectivity. These encompassed emerging areas of shared service such as Internet-based employee portals, finance and HR portals, knowledge-based portals and customer relationship management centers.

The powerful new idea behind the ISVV was that non-competing global corporations could establish a joint business incubator to explore and pilot new service platforms. Implicit in the arrangement was the commitment by these parties to pool their relational assets as a means of kick-starting new commercial businesses. For example, a total of one million staff employed by the potential sponsors could create critical mass for a shared HR portal.

The shared incubator would work with its sponsors to generate a stream of new marketplace opportunities and engage the appropriate senior executives in the business design and build activities. Equity ownership of the new businesses would be allocated to those sponsors willing to commit their internal markets as a means of generating liquidity. Financing would be readily available from the sponsors or other investment institutions given the attractiveness of the initial customer base.

Pre-occupation with the vertical markets impeded progress on implementing the original business model, but we are aware that some movement has taken place around this concept, and many more such ventures are likely in the coming months.

validated the partnering model. The steps that have been taken so far are small, and mostly inside the boundaries of the procurement function. The real benefits, and real challenges, come when these joint ventures jointly address new, and longer-term, opportunities.

Shared e-services appear to be the most immediate way of capitalizing on existing corporate assets and relationships. These services are designed to convert current business expense and know-how into shareholder value without threatening perceived competitive differentiation. Examples of these e-services would include the following:

- *E-HR portals*: we envisage establishing a common HR portal for employees across the partner organizations by integrating a range of HR services from "best-in-breed" suppliers. Each partner in this horizontal service provider would be able to customize the portal for its own purposes whilst enjoying the scope and coverage of a global capability. With the backing of ten or more major corporates, one million employees could be connected to this service, thus expanding scale and scope well beyond an individual partner's capability. By addressing the combined needs of one million or more employees across several major corporations, shared e-employee portals will be able to offer outstanding services ranging from comprehensive benefits management and flexible pension schemes to on-line training and life-long learning. They may also be able to generate opportunities for short work secondments amongst the portal partners. Early examples such as www.oneclickhr.com show the potential of a shared HR service, but they need corporate muscle to drive them.

- *E-customer care services*: this would establish common call centers across the geographic regions through which all consumer contact would take place. For many major corporates, the majority of customer contact today takes place with business customers rather than end-consumers. The aggregation of such consumer contact brings scale efficiencies as well as new prospects for data mining and direct marketing. Although they start as horizontal service providers, if the data were efficiently mined and re-used, these entities would have tremendous potential value as customer managers.

- *E-finance services:* some global corporations, such as Proctor & Gamble are well advanced in separating out back-office services into global units that integrate the needs of different business divisions. These e-services could be developed further into a service platform that supports other corporate customers. Through aggregation of demand, large "lights off" processing centers (e.g. largely unmanned facilities) can be created to serve the needs of the partners and other corporations, achieving new economies of scale and added value services.

- *E-knowledge in global trading:* to exploit valuable knowledge in international trading, we envisage the formation of an extranet able to assemble, chronicle and disseminate relevant commercial know-how. Most global corporations are experienced in dealing with over 200 different national environments, and have amassed knowledge of local laws, regulations and business conditions. A smart company such as this could be extended into other relevant knowledge domains.

- *Asset broking:* corporations within the same industry, whether it be bandwidth, refining, steel-making, pipelining or any similar industry, could make their capital assets available to an asset broker that could lease spare capacity and provide a futures market for known capacity shortfalls. This would be the first step towards the creation of large business platforms.

Associated with all the above propositions is the prospect of major consultancy activities required to transform current modes of operating to conform to new e-service capabilities. This would be an essential add-on service to any joint partnership.

By creating a small exclusive partnership amongst Global 2000 corporations, we believe that these corporations can exploit combined market liquidity to achieve critical mass in the new market spaces. The diversity and strength of their collective skills – or digital capital, in areas such as brand management, sales, HR, technology and process re-engineering will ensure world-class outcomes in each new shared business platform.

LEVERAGING COLLECTIVE RELATIONSHIPS

As we have explained, in the connected economy intangible assets like the relationships between businesses and trading partners take on central importance. In the first months of the digital economy, leading organizations have already applied partnering vehicles to exploit such new sources of shared value.

In the case of procurement, supplier–customer relationships are being securitized through the formation of vertical and horizontal marketplaces. Currently, billions of dollars of spend are being converted into future IPO value, as well as delivering millions of dollars of cost savings.

As we discovered in Chapter 6 there are numerous other relationships that could yield similar, high-value returns. As we shall see below, the spotlight will fall shortly on employee–employer relationships as shared Internet portals become conduits for benefits management, career choices and life-long learning. Thereafter, shared customer portals may offer vast new wealth creation opportunities (Fig. 12.3).

In addition to leveraging relationships, many of the more traditional corporate assets such as physical and virtual infrastructures – for example, physical assets and buildings, computers and networks, are being targeted for innovative new e-business propositions. Corporations contemplating large outsourcing deals are demanding equity swaps in addition to cost savings. Some are considering shared "operate" ventures where value can be retained and enhanced within an extended customer group.

COLLABORATION PRESENTS A NEW BUSINESS MODEL

The collaborative approach presents a new model for corporate venturing within the connected economy. By combining together the collective assets of the participating corporations, including their internal/external customers and individual competencies, the partnership of like-minded but complimentary corporations can launch e-market initiatives that maximize the common wealth of the participants to mutual advantage. This is particularly of advantage if a potential atom has the skills, but not the critical mass, to survive.

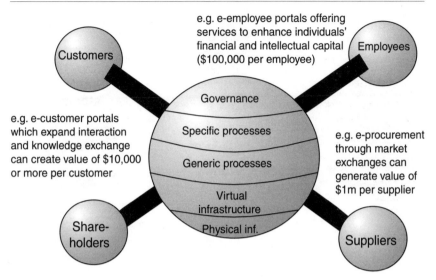

Figure 12.3 Value lies in securitizing relationships.

Speed to market will be a key success factor once the partnerships gain sufficient levels of mutual trust.

For many organizations, one of the factors that determines the speed of progress will be the rate at which managers can be trained to form relationships and build adaptive structures that minimize switching costs.

This structure for collaboration links the concept of an internal corporate venture with a shared think-tank. Founding members create an ongoing research and development program that identifies new marketplace opportunities and mobilizes the necessary internal stakeholders and resources to pursue the most attractive options (see Fig. 12.4).

In effect, such a partnership becomes a shared incubator that identifies, formulates and launches new marketplaces and atoms on behalf of its partners – not dissimilar to the internal incubators, or "e-labs," that many larger corporations operate today on behalf of their own business divisions.

HOW WILL THE MODEL OPERATE?

The proposed collaborative model brings together qualified communities of interest to brainstorm new propositions. For example, in the area of e-employee portals, senior HR directors from across the member organizations can work

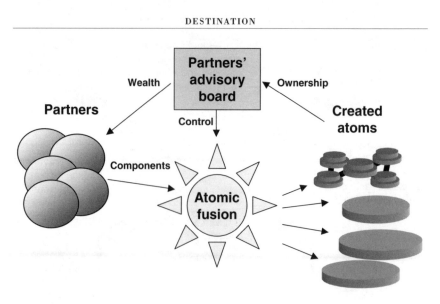

Figure 12.4 Collaborative structures.

together to anticipate the future needs and aspirations of their employees. Using workshops or forums, the joint venture vehicle can develop specific business models and propositions that can be offered back to the community of interest for validation and launch (see Fig. 12.5).

Attracting five or more world-leading collaborators into such a partnership, the prospects could be dramatic.

A shared incubator could capitalize on a possible customer base of a hundred thousand or more business partners, a million employees and over one hundred million end consumers.

The expanded connectivity inherent within this community could give rise to a broad range of enhanced services and associated sources of value added.

Such a partnership would be able to exploit a unique set of internal competencies ranging from consumer and brand leadership through to global business operations in 200 countries, and technology leadership. In this respect, the combined digital assets of the group would far exceed those of any individual member.

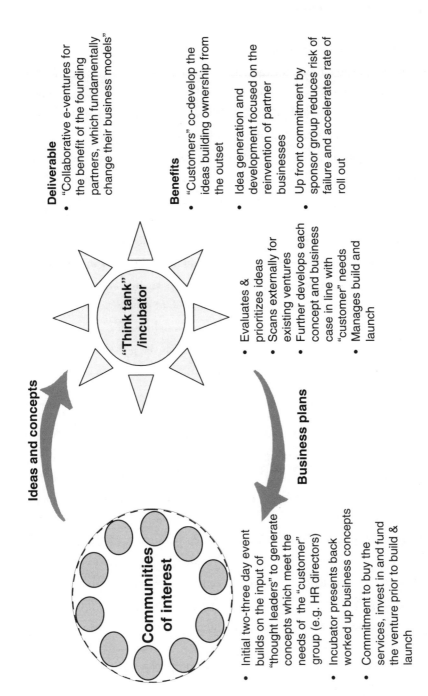

Deliverable

- "Collaborative e-ventures for the benefit of the founding partners, which fundamentally change their business models"

Benefits

- "Customers" co-develop the ideas building ownership from the outset
- Idea generation and development focused on the reinvention of partner businesses
- Up front commitment by sponsor group reduces risk of failure and accelerates rate of roll out

"Think tank"/incubator

- Evaluates & prioritizes ideas
- Scans externally for existing ventures
- Further develops each concept and business case in line with "customer" needs
- Manages build and launch

Ideas and concepts

Business plans

Communities of interest

- Initial two-three day event builds on the input of "thought leaders" to generate concepts which meet the needs of the "customer" group (e.g. HR directors)
- Incubator presents back worked up business concepts
- Commitment to buy the services, invest in and fund the venture prior to build & launch

Figure 12.5 Venture creation process.

From thought to commercialization

Through the combined assets and commercial potential of such a co-operative vehicle, the partnership can expect to raise external capital, where needed, for its ventures at a very competitive rate. The partnership and its associated ventures should also contribute a "halo" effect to the stock market valuation of its partners by generating a broad range of future growth options.

Of greatest appeal however will be the relationships created between the corporate members themselves. These will enable the consortium, in effect a *virtual keiretsu*, to be first to market with new e-propositions by avoiding the need to search exhaustively for partners each time round.

As a shared incubator, the partnership is designed to identify and pursue emerging e-market and e-service opportunities wherever they make sense to the members. Its mandate is to exploit the common wealth of the consortium to generate a stream of business innovations that yield exceptional value. To be successful here it must also assume the role of thought leader, anticipating the major trends in new e-propositions such as e-employee portals.

Conditions to create a successful consortium

With over two years of experience in brokering such ventures, we recognize that chief executive sponsorship is a pre-requisite to achieving closure for a global consortium. Only the CEO has the authority to commit both the corporate assets (employees, business partners and end consumers) and internal competencies necessary to enable the partnership to succeed.

A second prerequisite is to find partner corporations with the appropriate corporate style to harness their combined internal assets. Those corporations with relatively decentralized structures and cultures will find great difficulty in mobilizing the necessary assets to contribute effectively to a joint venture. A centralized corporate structure is essential to build the necessary liquidity into new e-marketplaces and e-services.

Functional heads such as chief financial officers, directors of HR and chief marketing officers will need to be engaged directly in the development of individual propositions to ensure alignment of best practice and to secure access to the necessary internal customers. For example, in the development of an e-employee portal, HR directors would need to participate in a brainstorming exercise to co-develop a shared portal proposition. The joint incubator team would then refine the initial proposition and cycle it back to the sponsor group for validation and approval.

Mobilizing support for a collaborative venture

The task of winning corporate-wide support for a major joint venture is highly challenging. Our experience suggests that a senior executive – possibly the head of e-business – should be deployed full time to kick off the new model. The tasks involved would include:

- assisting in gaining CEO and other relevant top-line executive approval within the sponsor organization;
- helping establish a shared incubator with a full team of business and technology staff on the ground;
- kicking off initial venture planning processes and prototyping exercises in league with other sponsors; and
- formalizing governance principles for the partnership including share holdings and financial support.

What will be the pay-off for collaborative ventures?

A collaborative venture such as the one described above requires a relatively modest commitment of resource by each individual partner of around two million dollars and two to three seconded staff in the first year of operation. But the investment opens up unique opportunities to play in the new economy. As new ventures emerge from the shared incubator, each partner buys the option to make an investment – thus expanding its future growth options. A likely flow of ventures would be one qualifying new business per quarter.

By creating such growth options, each organization might benefit in four important ways. They might:

■ secure early mover access to new e-transformation techniques and e-services that incorporate best-in-class thinking from across many different industry sectors;

■ convert "internal expense to value" through the development of shared e-services that transfer internal non-core assets and processes to an external vehicle;

■ generate valuable equity investments in new commercial ventures that will expand well beyond the charter members' combined internal markets; and

■ develop a "halo" effect in the eyes of the world's stock markets through unique association with prestige brands and business entities.

As we stated earlier, there are few such ventures currently in operation. But we expect to see many emerge in the course of the next few years as corporations seek to securitize their relationships and other assets through collaborative schemes.

SUMMARY

Effective co-operation and collaboration are key ambitions of atomization. You won't survive in the connected economy without them. And that is why we think they are vital to the early stage of atomization. It provides, in effect, a relatively safe way of starting the wrecking ball swinging. Employees and shareholders won't be unduly frightened by what might have been described in the past as a joint venture but should in fairly quick time demonstrate the value of relational capital.

You may not get it right first time. But a move towards collaboration is a move towards survival. The new economy demands a mindset of agility rather than efficiency and that transformation is enabled by collaboration.

We have now seen how large corporations, including the one you work for, can release enormous value as part of their effort to prepare for the new economy. But we hope also to have prepared you for the future by explaining where the change is coming from and what it will mean for existing corporate structures. Our next and final chapter will speculate about what all this will mean for you as an individual, outside the environs of the office.

PART V
Destiny

We have seen how large corporations, including the one you work for, can release tremendous value by identifying and releasing specialist atoms. It's time for a bold move. We know that you won't get it right first time (and even if you do, the situation will have changed), so survival in this new economy demands a mindset not of efficiency but of agility. Check the conditions, do it, learn from it, check the conditions, do it again.

But the most important section of this book is the one you are about to read – what it means to you as an individual. We are all about to find out what that old Chinese proverb about "living in interesting times" really means. Welcome to the world of portfolio careers, the household COO and the first trillionaire.

CHAPTER 13

The Atomized Individual

CONFRONTING OUR DESTINY

W E THINK THE FORCES OF CHANGE that we have described up to now are going to be so profound that their impact will be felt well beyond just the corporate orbit. That's why we will conclude by applying some of our atomic model to the level of the individual and speculate about what it will mean for our daily existence. You may choose to dismiss it as a flight of fancy but we hope it will at least provide you with some food for thought about what the business world of tomorrow holds in store.

SETTING THE INDIVIDUAL CONTEXT

Our atomic model predicts that corporations will fragment into lots of different pieces, from "smart companies" consisting of a handful of creative engineers and designers to "asset platforms" involving global operations and billions of dollars of capital. These "atomic" structures will be bound together by electronic markets whose role is to connect many commercial partners together into infinitely variable value networks.

The atomic model strongly reflects corporate competencies such as product design, customer management, deal-making and operational support. One size does not fit all, and companies will need to select a specific area of competence if they are to develop a valuable role in the connected economy. We feel that the same arguments could be applied to the individual, who is the most vital and flexible atomic component of any economic system.

Living and working in an atomized economy, you will have far greater choices to make. You will need to establish just where you think your specialization lies and where you fit into the new atomic structure. It won't necessarily be an easy decision but there will be some comfort in the scale of reward that will be offered by the atomic corporation.

WELCOME TO THE NEW TRILLENNIUM

In our view a more appropriate name for the new millennium would be the "trillennium" because we predict that within the next ten years the world will see its first trillionaire. It won't be Bill Gates or Larry Ellison. In fact, it won't be anyone featured on the pages of today's *Fortune* magazine, the *Financial Times*, or *Wall Street Journal*. Instead, we think our first trillionaire is still at high school, still blissfully unaware of his or her brilliant prospects.

Where is this mega wealth going to come from? Connectivity in the global village. With the new era of visual and virtual communications, the prospects for interaction here are almost boundless, and so too are the rewards for innovative new applications and services that exploit this connectivity. We are living in a world of increasing returns and these could be literally unbounded as networks reach near infinite proportions.

GREATER INDIVIDUAL CHOICE

Ask a prosperous parent of the post-war generation what aspirations they had for their children and the response would most likely be one of the professions. Medicine, law or accountancy. Fifty years on the answer is no longer so simple. For a start, there are hundreds of occupations that now have something like the traditional professions, whether it be management consultancy, IT systems design or alternative health care.

But more importantly, this upsurge in choice brings with it greater individual responsibility. There may be more variety in today's job market but there is correspondingly less security. And we expect that diminution of job security to accelerate in the future. After all, one of the defining features of the atomic corporation is its adaptability and an inviolably tenured workforce is antithetical to its capacity to withstand the winds of change. So don't look for the atomized corporations to have your welfare at heart. It is still the case that employment contracts in continental Europe average sixteen years – thanks to the region's more enduringly traditional social protection laws. Compare that to Silicon Valley, where the average employment contract is now down to eighteen months. We expect that in years to come employment contracts will average thirty days, based on a continuous process of re-negotiation between employer and employee.

WEALTH ACCUMULATION – ASPIRATION OR NECESSITY?

The other dimension that has changed distinctly since the last century is the time constraints on earning capacity. During much of the industrial age a career was measured in continuous periods of 30–40 years. Many pension schemes still reflect this legacy. We think the extraordinary demands of tomorrow's business and professional life could further truncate full-time employment to the point where the millennium generation should plan on retirement at forty, with some 10–20 further years spent in portfolio occupations.

That may sound daunting but there's an upside. Remuneration has outstripped inflation for most jobs in the last twenty years to the point where real incomes are at least double those of our parents. The prospect of a million-dollar salary is not unrealistic for anyone reading this book. Indeed, we hope that many of you will enjoy rewards well in excess of this figure for sustained periods of ten or more years. And that cash flow will be used not just to finance today's living expenses but tomorrow's leisure time. In effect, we will need to build a personal investment engine to cover our entire life cycle needs.

But don't expect anyone to be looking after your interests. Even Europe's more leftist governments have begrudgingly acknowledged the unsustainability of wide-scale public pension provision. It's up to you, and you alone in the new atomic world. Even the family unit is tenuous. According to US government statistics in 1960, the average household consisted of salaried male, housewife and two children. Today less than five percent of US households conform to that description. Similarly, in the UK over a third of house transactions are undertaken by single people. Each one of us will need to take charge of our own destiny. The process of individualization is well and truly underway.

WHO DO WE WANT TO BE?

It is often said in the consulting profession that the long climb to partner or vice-president status is based on a combination of the following attributes:

- *Rainmaker* – someone with the ability to drum up exceptional business even in the most unlikely circumstances. An hour spent in an airport lounge talking to a perfect stranger may lead to a million-dollar sales opportunity! The winning characteristics here are charisma and creativity.
- *Relationship manager* – an expert at creating and sustaining working relationships with clients that are built on trust and personal chemistry. They often turn out to be the most productive means of generating new business. This requires commitment and focus. For many firms, client relationships today can be measured in the tens of millions of dollars.
- *Program manager* – someone masterfully organized. They can be trusted to undertake complex and risky projects. If the program manager says its Christmas tomorrow – you better believe it.
- *Subject matter expert* – a leader and an expert in a field based on literally years studying an industry or technology to minute detail to become a recognized thought leader and expert in the subject. It was said of one famous IBM watcher that he knew what the CEO of IBM had eaten for breakfast – and could relate this to share price fluctuations during the day!

We can't excel in all these areas – many of them are mutually exclusive. But the secret to success is to recognize and build on strengths whilst complementing weaknesses. Strong professional practices will employ a combination of the above skills – embodied in different individuals but carefully orchestrated by the senior partner, or "portfolio owner."

This is individual atomization, the personal counterpart to the corporate phenomenon.

AN ATOMIC CLASSIFICATION

We can see a close correspondence between the individual characteristics described above and our corporate atoms. The relationship manager is the "customer manager" in our corporate universe, able to develop an intimate understanding of an individual client. The value created here can be exceptional in personal equity terms, and has lasting impact.

The subject-matter expert corresponds to the "smart company" category, and is an accumulator and broker of intellectual capital rather like a successful design shop. Sensitivity to change in the external environment is a critical dimension here, and we can expect such individuals to ride the crest of several waves in their careers. The rainmaker is also closely linked to the smart company, given that success in creating new relationships and business ideas depends on personal creativity and agility.

The webspinner is the program manager or "orchestrator" who knows how to bring together resources to undertake a complex assignment and achieve a stretched target. Relationships are important here, but the skill of teaming together a diversity of skills to achieve a result is the critical underlying competence.

In the dynamic and rapidly changing future, our focus will be on achieving excellence in one or at most two of the above categories. We may, for example, gain academic qualifications and practical experience in one specific area for many years to become a thought leader and world-class practitioner. But whichever course we chose to take, one thing is abundantly clear about the road ahead – it will require years of intense effort and fierce competition to reach a sustainable level of proficiency, and the huge bundles of dollars that go with it.

WHO WILL MANAGE THE BACK OFFICE OF OUR LIVES?

How do we expect to manage our lives in the intervening period? Or for that matter once we have climbed to the dizzy heights of personal success? Some of us may be lucky enough to acquire a life partner who is prepared to accept the role of being the chief operating officer of the household. But as the gender barriers throughout business are gradually eroded further these will become an endangered species.

So the answer is to outsource our back office to credible partners like financial organizations. We will be seeking support at several levels, and in each area we can foresee lucrative service platforms emerging to cater for individual need. What are these basic needs?

- *Accommodation for life* – too much of our time and energy is spent today purchasing, fitting out and managing our domestic environment. How about a Regus Office approach to home dwellings? We buy a timeshare that entitles us to a roof over our heads – anywhere, any place, anytime across the world. We then alternate between capital cities whilst at work and country homes during leisure periods.

- *Mobility for life* – again much is made of acquiring and owning a car, be it a Ford Fiesta or Ferrari. For many city dwellers a car is a liability as much as an asset. Many of the world's leading car manufacturers are planning to provide mobility on demand as a more convenient solution to car ownership. This would enable us to choose different models for various times in the week, from a four-wheel drive or family saloon to a soft top sports.

- *Career for life* – managing our own personal capital is far too important to be left in non-specialist hands – and that includes our own. Some of the more progressive search firms are already piloting new schemes where they will contract with talented individuals for life, and lease them to attractive employers – to extract a high return both in income and capital gains. Already talent agencies ranging from fashion models to business gurus have adopted a similar approach where they take ownership of an individual's intellectual output in its many guises.

- *Health for life* – one of the most important dimensions of life in the fast track is personal health and well being. There is an exploding industry that offers us keep-fit and body overhauls. However, the majority of expenditure today is geared towards fixing problems once they have occurred, as per the medical profession. Who visits a doctor in full health? Again, we expect you will outsource personal well being to experts who will carry out continuous programs of self-improvement and disease prevention. Maybe we can look forward to a new generation of designer drugs to control appetite, slow down ageing and increase energy levels.

The commercial opportunities presented here feed back well into our atomic corporation. Service providers will need to form one-to-one relationships with individuals to deliver on the above promises, and employ webspinners to collect together the numerous products and services necessary to realize these personalized offers. In turn, each individual will need to trust the provider sufficiently to exchange personal and confidential information on their intimate life patterns. We will come to regard such information exchanges as an investment of personal intellectual property from which we will expect ample rewards.

AND SO TO THE FUTURE

So how can we best prepare for the atomic world ahead? As frequently stated, the rewards for getting it right will be enormous. But the penalties for failure both in our work and domestic lives will also never be greater.

We will need to identify and build on our core competencies as individuals from an early age, and receive guidance from experts to help us to maximize our personal wealth. We will also need to engage with complementary talents and skills to create effective teams both in our work and social settings. And we will need to place our trust in external agencies that will take on an ever-increasing proportion of our day-to-day existence – our personal back office.

Does this sound utopian? Possibly. But you can't ignore the powerful forces of change that will shape your life in the future.

In the words of American futurist Watts Wacker:

> *"How you organize the future has an awful lot to do with what you do with it … an optimist tends to have a pretty good future and a pessimist has a pretty bad one, but interestingly they can have exactly the same thing happen to them."*

Notes

FOREWORD

1 *The Innovator's Dilemma*, Clayton Christensen, Harvard Business School Press, 1997. ISBN 0875845851

CHAPTER 2

1 Karl Marx (perhaps the greatest management consultant of the nineteenth century) proposed an entirely new economic model based on the elimination of capital. His experiment worked well for a while, but failed to include a market mechanism. Since there was no external transaction cost to balance against, the sizes of the economic entities and the internal costs soared. In short, it was bound to fail, although we concede that there may have been other factors involved in the fall of Communism.

2 Oliver E. Williamson, (1967) "Hierarchical control and optimum firm size," *Journal of Political Economy* 75:123–138.

3 Coase, Ronald H. (1937) "The nature of the firm," *Economica N.S.* 4:386–405.

4 An excellent annotated bibliography of Transaction Cost Economics has been prepared by Professor Harvey S. James and can be found in the Scout Report for Social Sciences, Scout Project 1994–2000 at http://scout.cs.wisc.edu/, or at a variety of other Web sites. Try http://uhavax.hartford.edu/~hjames/tce-bib.html or http://www.economy.boom.ru/pubs/bib.htm.

5 Oliver E. Williamson, (1975) *Markets and Hierarchies: Analysis and Antitrust Implications: A Study in the Economics of Internal Organization,*

Free Press, New York, ISBN 0029347807, and (1985) *The Economic Institutions of Capitalism: Firms, Markets, Relational Contracting*, New York: Free Press, ISBN 0029348218.

6   This list of reasons for merger is taken from *Successful Business Acquisition*, by Smith and Sadtler, Delta Sierra Publishing, 2000, ISBN 0953916200. We are grateful for their kind permission to reproduce this list.

7   Sometime corporations are too small on their own. For example, an automobile corporation must produce about 2m cars per year for efficient operation, forcing Volvo, which made 400,000 cars per year, to find a buyer (source as note 6).

8   Michael Porter, *Harvard Business Review*, May–June, 1987.

9   *The Net-Ready Organisation*, Sharon Voros. This is available from www.cisco.com.

10   Electronic Data Interchange, an early form of e-commerce involving fixed-format messages defined by standards such as ANSI X12 and UN EDIFACT, proved difficult and costly to install and maintain, although fairly efficient once operating. Modern standards such as Extensible Markup Language (XML) offer the same benefits and increased flexibility at lower cost.

11   Quoted in Tapscott, Ticoll, and Lowy's *Digital Capital*, ISBN 1857882091, p. 8.

12   We will demonstrate in Chapter 8 that most of the e-markets formed in 2000 and 2001 are likely to collapse over the next two years. The successors to the current rash of vertical marketplaces will concentrate on process, not procurement, so the question is one of timing rather than effect.

CHAPTER 3

1   *Blur*, Stan Davies and Christopher Meyer. Published by Perseus/Capstone, Oxford, 1998, ISBN 1841120820.

2   *Reengineering the Corporation*, Michael Hammer and James Champy. Published by HarperBusiness, 1993, ISBN 0887306403.

CHAPTER 6

1   From *The Discipline of Market Leaders* by Micheal Treacy and Fred Wiersema. Published by Perseus Press, 1997. ISBN 0201407191.

CHAPTER 7

1   Enron's shareholder briefing, Jan 2000.

2   Quote from Tim Koogle, chairman and CEO of Yahoo! in his FY2000 analyst briefing.

3   We would definitely expect the best recruitment and executive search agencies to become customer managers.

4   Philip Evans and Thomas Wurster have discussed at length what they describe as the logic of affiliation. At the moment, customer managers (they use the term "navigators") affiliate with sellers because richness of content tends to be specific to suppliers, and because consumers are unwilling to pay for advice. They argue that the use of rich communications channels will see a shift to buyer affiliation as it represents a major competitive advantage for the customer manager. We would agree with that. See *Blown to Bits*, by Philips Evans and Thomas Wurster, Harvard Business School Press, ISBN 087584877, pp. 129ff.

5   Tesco is blurring the line between retailing and banking by allowing its customers to pay their household bills at the checkout

CHAPTER 8

1   Liquidity is the ability to turn your assets into cash on demand. If there is not enough business going through a marketplace, it cannot work efficiently. This applies as much to stock exchanges as to indirect procurement marketplaces.

2   E-procurement is perhaps an idea which had the best value proposition of any e-commerce initiative – not just because it reduced internal and external transaction costs but because it was a way to introduce good sourcing practice into the organizations. Unfortunately, we saw many

companies approach e-procurement systems as a technology problem, not a sourcing problem, and the results were often dismal.

3   Forrester Research, "The eMarketplace Shakeout," August 2000. Available to subscribers from www.forrester.com.

4   See www.covisint.com for details.

5   "Neutrality is important," said BMW executive Wilhelm Becker in June 2000, "Covisint is too controlled by our friends in America. We don't want to see our secrets in the hands of our competitors. Covisint is not neutral enough." Quoted in *Business 2.0*, January 2001.

6   Cisco's virtual manufacturing process can be seen as a "private" vertical. In *Digital Capital*, Tapscott, Ticoll. and Lowy have made an interesting, although complex, distinction between types of marketplace along axes of degree of value added and whether dominated or self-organizing. The marketplaces we propose do not readily fit these categories, but Tapscott *et al* would recognize our service platform as an "aggregation" and our verticals as "value chains" or "distributive networks" depending on the degree of independence. See Don Tapscott, David Ticoll, Alex Lowy, (2000) *Digital Capital*, Nicholas Brealey Publishing Ltd, ISBN 1857882091.

7   The problem is not so much the agreed standard – although deciding which dialect of XML will win is challenge enough – as the implementation of the standards in all of the players in the supply chain and the deep integration of electronic messaging into their systems. Far too many EDI links ended at a PC or printer, and the large players will this time need to insist on integration into the suppliers' systems if responsiveness is to be guaranteed.

8   Regulators are looking closely at vertical marketplaces to ensure that they do not distort the structure of the industry by combining to force down prices. The regulators will find it harder to stop horizontal marketplaces from aggregating the spend of their members, and so the horizontal marketplaces should offer significant price advantages.

9   We will not speculate what the situation will change to, but it is difficult to foresee how we can have a common global taxation system without at least an element of common global government.

CHAPTER 9

1   *Blown to Bits*, Philip Evans and Thomas Wurster, Harvard Business School Press, ISBN 087584877, p. 222.

CHAPTER 10

1   We say only a little, because now that discovery and sourcing costs are near zero, only the switching cost stops re-alliance. To maximize flexibility and minimize the chances of long-term survival, the atoms must keep the switching cost low. So don't let them get too close!

2   Adam Smith, *An Enquiry into the Nature and Causes of the Wealth of Nations*. Modern Library, ISBN 0679783369.

3   Quotation from Mainspring Consulting's paper, "New skills for the new economy: a primer on partnerships and alliances," September 2000. Available from www.mainspring.com.

4   Just dividing the cost of the AP function by the number of transactions that it handles, for example, gives you an estimate of the current internal cost. This is *not* the same as an estimate of the potential revenue of the function.

5   Don't yell at us or send us nasty e-mails telling us of all the deep flaws in the P/E ratio (e.g. it misrepresents the value of companies which are debt-ridden or which operate tax-minimization schemes) – we know all that, but it is the ratio the market tends to use, flawed or not.

6   We used FTSE Industry Indices. You could perform the same calculation based on Dow Jones SIC codes, and get much the same result.

7   Figures for asset platforms are based on companies from the automobile, energy, mining, aerospace & defense, construction, transport, chemicals, electricity, engineering, forestry, paper and packaging industries.

8   The variability, where we have a large enough sample of industries, is based on one standard deviation from the mean.

9   Figures for horizontal service platforms are based on 208 companies from the support services, health, real estate, hotels, banks, distributors, life assurance, insurance and finance industries.

10   Figures for portfolio owners are based on the FTSE index of 127 invest-
      ment companies.

11   Figures for smart companies are based on the FTSE index of 72 soft-
      ware and computer services companies. This is far from an ideal sample,
      hence the wider spread.

12   *Break-up!* by David Sadtler, Andrew Campbell (Contributor), Richard
      Koch. Published by Free Press, 1997, ISBN 0684845105.

CHAPTER 11

1   These are generally standard indirect procurement services, but some
      of the more aggressive banks are also offering purchase-to-payment pro-
      cesses using ERP systems – these are already on the way to becoming
      horizontal service platforms.

2   Markets, in this sense, include stock exchanges, money markets, cur-
      rency exchanges, commodity markets, and the associated derivatives
      markets.

3   LevelSeas is an atom created by Shell to link those who have
      freight to carry with ship owners who have spare capacity. See
      www.levelseas.com.

4   OceanConnect is an exchange for marine fuel, centered around Shell's
      storage and distribution facilities. See www.oceanconnect.com for de-
      tails.

5   Auctions held in 2000 and 2001 in several European countries lumbered
      telcos who wished to operate 3G (third generation mobile) services with
      very high license costs, while license auctions in other countries effec-
      tively failed due to lack of bidders. Although Europe is perhaps two years
      ahead of the US in mobile communications, the introduction of 3G there
      appears to be facing a period of uncertainty.

Selected Glossary

Bandwidth   Refers to a communication medium's capacity to carry data and transactions. Low bandwidth links (such as twisted pair) generally carry voice traffic, while high bandwidth links can carry video, tele-presence etc. traffic.

Bluetooth   Bluetooth is a computing and telecommunications industry specification that allows devices to connect with each other via a short-range wireless connection. Provides reasonably high bandwidth over a range of about ten meters. Named after Harald Bluetooth, a 10th century Danish king who united the Scandinavian tribes.

Broadband   Telecommunications links that provide multiple channels of data over a single communications medium.

Coaxial cable   Cable that includes one physical channel (generally copper wire) within a layer of insulation and another concentric physical channel (generally copper mesh), both running along the same axis. The outer channel serves as a ground. Low cost, and can carry information for a great distance. Depending on the carrier technology used and other factors, twisted pair copper wire and optical fiber are alternatives to coaxial cable.

Direct goods   Goods that are purchased by corporations for inclusion in their end products – for an automobile company, these would be steel, tires, glass, seats, computer chips etc.

Dividend yield   A measure of the profit per share that a corporation returns to its owners. Calculated as gross dividend divided by the share price.

Electronic Data Interchange   EDI (Electronic Data Interchange) is a first generation e-commerce language developed in the 1960s. Large companies and their significant trading partners constructed costly proprietary systems that "spoke" to each other in EDI dialects, usually ANSI X12 or

UN EDIFACT. Unlike XML, EDI was only capable of supporting fixed format messages. Efficient, but inflexible.

Fiber optic   Fiber optic (or "optical fiber") is a technology associated with the transmission of information as light impulses along a glass or plastic fiber. Fiber optic wire carries much more information than conventional copper wire and is far less subject to interference. Most telephone company long-distance lines are now fiber optic.

Indirect goods   Goods which are purchased by corporations which are not included in their end products, but which are necessary to keep operating – for an automobile company, these would be IT systems, flights, furniture, tools etc.

IPO   Initial Public Offering. Placing a large number shares in a (usually) fledgling corporation on a stock exchange in order to obtain capital for growth or to create a liquid market in the shares.

ISDN   Integrated Services Digital Network (ISDN) is a set of standards for high-speed digital transmission of voice and data over ordinary telephone copper wire. It is capable of transmitting at speeds of up to 128Kbps.

ISP   Internet Service Provider. Usually a link between a home user and the Internet.

Liquidity   The ability for participants in a marketplace (physical and electronic) to convert their assets into cash, and vice versa. Liquidity is essential if the marketplace is to attract new buyers and sellers.

Marketplace   In the sense of this book, a marketplace is a Web site that facilitates trade between corporations. Marketplaces are generally divided into *verticals*, which address industry-specific trade, or *horizontals*, which provide a range of services or processes to clients regardless of their industry. By aggregating buyers and sellers (i.e. providing liquidity) and by automating paper-based workflows, well-executed marketplaces should reduce prices and transaction costs. Examples include CoVisint (an automotive vertical) and CoNext (a procurement horizontal).

MP3   MP3 (MPEG-1, audio layer 3) is a standard format for compressing a sound sequence into a very small file (about one-twelfth the size of the original file) while preserving a level of sound quality similar to the original.

NPV   Net Present Value. A method of calculating the value, in today's terms, of a cost or investment made at some point in the future. Similar to the concept of compound interest.

P/E ratio   A measure of the faith of a group of investors in a corporation's shares, reflecting how many years the investors would have to hold the shares to get their money back. Measured as the ratio of the share price to the per-share earnings, where earnings are calculated after taxes, depreciation, interest etc. have been deducted, or the total market capitalization of the company divided by its after-tax (etc.) profit.

PDA   Personal Digital Assistant. A hand-held computer.

Permanent establishment   The country or state in which a corporation is located for taxation purposes. Usually consists of an office, a showroom etc. The concept of permanent establishment is blurred by Web-only enterprises.

Portal   A portal is a Web site that users tend to visit as a means of accessing other sites and content. Portals can be general (AOL, Yahoo! MSN) or support niche interests (garden.com, ivillage.com). Typical services offered by portals include a directory of Web sites, a facility to search for other sites, news, weather information, e-mail, stock quotes, phone and map information, and sometimes a community forum.

Real options   A mechanism for estimating the value of an investment based on a series of yes/no decisions made at some point in the future, generally based on unexpected market developments. Works well where there is widespread uncertainty in markets.

Re-engineering   Often referred to as "process re-engineering." A mechanism for looking at the means by which a corporation operates with the intention of merging parts of the process, eliminating steps, and reducing costs. Popularized by Champy and Hammer's book "Re-engineering the Corporation," it was common in the 1980s and 1990s.

Relational capital   Relational capital is term coined by the authors to describe a growing source of shareholder value derived from longstanding relationships with key business stakeholders (e.g. customers, suppliers). Value is created through the continuing interaction (both financial and informational) between a company and its valued stakeholders.

Shareholder value   The wealth that a corporation generates for its shareholders. Composed of dividends and capital growth.

Tele-presence   The transmission of stereoscopic vision and feedback for mechanical movement between remote locations to allow interaction at the remote site (e.g. surgery).

Transaction cost   The cost incurred when dealing with another party, in addition to the price of the goods. Usually consists of discovery costs (deciding what you are going to buy and who from), sourcing costs (contracting and buying), and policing costs (ensuring the contract is met).

Transaction cost economics   Transaction cost economics is a school of economic theory, which looks at the way in which institutions are affected by the balances between the costs of different ways of doing business, and the nature of formal and informal contracts.

Transfer pricing   Payments from one part of a multinational enterprise to another part for goods or services provided.

Twisted pair   Twisted pair is the link that traditionally connects homes and small-business computers to the telephone company. It is composed of two insulated copper wires, which are twisted around each other.

UMTS   Universal Mobile Telecommunications System is a third-generation (3G) broadband wireless transmission standard. It will offer text, voice, video, and multimedia services to mobile computer and phone users.

Vertical integration   Buying corporations which supply you with direct materials or which distribute your products. A once popular means of reducing prices and ensuring free flow of physical goods. The need for vertical integration is largely eliminated by improving the parallel information flows.

WAP   Wireless Application Protocol is a (largely European) low-bandwidth communications protocol designed to provide interactive access to mobile phone users.

Index

Accenture 33
Alcatel 68
Amazon.com 46, 75, 81, 82, 103, 149
America Online (AOL) 75
Amoco 80
AOL Time Warner 76
Apple computers 47
Arthur D Little 33
asset platform 10, 13, 98, 199
    atomization opportunities 161, 166,
        167, 169–70, 172, 174
    characteristics 105–6
    questions concerning 139
    strategy 168, 176
AT&T 71, 169
Atomic Corporation
    advantages 127
    analysis 136
        asset platform 139
        customer manager 138
        example 139–41
        service platform 139
        smart company 138–9
        webspinner 138
    brand protection 149–50
    business plan 156–7
    characteristics 127–8
    competencies 147–8
    configuration 141, 143
    future possibilities 205
    identifying elements 135–6
    input/output linkage 141, 142
    layers 132–5
        asset-based platform 135
        governance 135
        service platform 135

    specific business elements 135
    management 146–7
    new collaborative approach 184
    obstacles 157
    organization chart 137
    profitability 151
    relationship management 148–9
    root and branch process 143
    sharing benefits 145–6
    size 144–5
    skills portfolio 146
    value 151–6
    viability 150–51
atomic industry
    asset/service platforms 176
    banking and insurance 160–64
    consumer products 171–3
    customer manager 176
    energy sector 164–8
    future possibilities 177, 205
    information technology 173–6
    smart companies 176
    strategies 158–60
        customer intimacy 159
        operational excellence 158
        product innovation 158–9
    telecommunications operators
        168–71
atoms 3–4, 10–12
    assets 10–11
    capital 11
    constituent parts 98–110
    future of 110–12
    innovation 10
    introduction to 96–8
    origins 12–14

relationships 10
working in world of 124–6

Bank of Scotland 88
banking and insurance (retail) 160, 162
    atomization opportunities
        asset platforms 161
        financial services retailer 161
        portfolio owners 161
        product innovators 161
        service offer integrators 161
        service platforms 161
banking (wholesale and corporate)
        162–3, 164
    atomization opportunities
        customer/relationship managers
            163
        market transaction engines 163–4
        portfolio owners 164
        syndication specialists 163
        transaction processing 163
Barclays Bank 80
Bell, Alexander Graham 39
Bluestone software 174
BMW 86
bonds 14, 99–100, 124
Booz Allen Hamilton 33
BP 165, 178
brand management 149–50
British Telecom 71, 88
Buffett, Warren 63, 64
Burroughs 68
business networks 79, 86–9
Business in The Third Millenium pro-
        gram 78, 80
business-to-business (B2B) 34–6, 37,
        99–100
business-to-consumer (B2C) 75
buying clubs 121

Cable & Wireless 170
cable corporations 68–9
Camrass, Roger 80
Cap Gemini Ernst & Young 33, 64, 78,
        179, 184

capital-intensive business 26
CDC 68
Chambers, John 51
Chevron 80, 165
Cisco Connection Online (CCO) 87
Cisco Employee Connection (CEO) 87
Cisco Manufacturing Connection Online
        (MCO) 87
Cisco Systems 31, 51, 68, 69, 86–7,
        174
Clarke, Jim 75
clickpaper.com 102
co-development 40–41
Coase Equilibrium 27
Coca-Cola Corporation 40, 86, 115–16,
        159, 166, 171, 172
collaborative approach *see* partnerships
communications 35, 39, 120
    media processor 52–3
    personal 50–51
    verbal–visual–virtual 53–7
community 44–5
Compaq 47
CoNext 121
connected economy 7–8, 38–9, 82–3
    corporate initiatives 178–80
        change the game 180
        create the new 180
        protect the core 180
    cost 57–9
    partnerships 184–94
consultants 31, 32–3, 34, 75, 99, 163
consumer products 171–2
    atomization opportunities
        design shops 172
        divestments 172
        lifestyle portals 172
Corning Glass 89
corporate center 182–3
corporation
    business elements
        generic 13, 130–31
        specific 12–13, 129–30
    capabilities
        customer intimacy 111, 159

organization excellence 111,
158–9
product innovation 111, 158
collaborations 184
decoupling competency/focus 97–8
forces of change 9–10
future role of center 182–3
governance 12, 128–9
initiatives 178–80
mergers 28–31
new governance models 180–81
corporate level 181–2
divisional level 182
operating unit level 182
new technology 34–6
organizational agility/creativity
89–90
physical infrastructure 13, 132
production-demand link 97
re-engineering 31–2, 34
reasons for formation
cost of doing business 23–5
internal costs 27–8
need for capital 25–6
supply chains 28
vertical integration 25–6
relationships 79–82
size 8–9, 36, 95
unchanging 6–7
virtual infrastructure 13, 131–2
Covisint 119, 184
customer 81
care services 186
changing 4–6
contact 35
understanding 97
value propositions
customer intimacy 85, 159
operational excellence 85
product leadership 85
customer manager 12, 13, 15, 98, 125,
172
atomization opportunities 161, 163,
166, 169, 172, 174
characteristics 102–3

individual classification 203
questions concerning 138
strategy 168, 176

Daewoo 88
DaimlerChrysler 119
Davis, Stan 82
Dell 85
destroy.coms 74
Deutsche Telecom 69
Digital 47
Disney 86
Dixon, Mark 107
dot.coms 74–7, 81, 179
Duke Energy 170

e-business-connected economy combination
challenge 178, 182–3
complexity 180–82
inertia 183
marketplace consolidation 179
new collaborative approach 184–94
patterns of approach 179–80
e-commerce 9, 34–6, 37, 100
e-employee portals 186, 189–90, 192,
193
e-HR portals 84, 86, 186
e-initiatives 178–80
e-procurement 114, 121
e-services 186–7, 192
Eastman Chemical 168
EDS 121
electronic data interchanges (EDI) 34
electronic markets 83–4
employment contracts 15
energy sector
atomization opportunities
(downstream)
global refining systems 167
knowledge based 167
market makers 166–7
service retailers 166
atomization opportunities (upstream)
shared asset/service platforms 166

smart companies 166
Enron 101–2, 167, 170
EnronCredit 101
EnronOnline 101
EPRI 80
Ericsson 51
ERP systems 32, 36, 171
European Commission 80
expectation gap 183
Expedia.com 43
Exxon 165

FirstMatter LLC 80
Ford Motor Company 25, 26, 88, 105,
    119, 149
France Telecom 69

Gartner and Forrester 163
Gas Research Council 80
gas sector *see* energy sector
General Electric 10
General Motors 73, 105, 119
GlaxoSmithKline 107
globalization 40, 123
    e-knowledge 187
Goldman Sachs 163

Hewlett, Bill 175
Hewlett-Packard 74, 174, 175, 183

IBM 38, 46, 47, 73, 174
Index 33
individual
    atomization opportunities
        program manager 202, 203
        rainmaker 202, 203
        relationship manager 202, 203
        subject matter expert 202, 203
    context 199–200
    future possibilities 205
    greater choice 200–201
    power 45–8, 59
    service platforms 203–5
        accommodation for life 204
        career for life 204

health for life 204
mobility for life 204
wealth accumulation 201
information 45–6
    intimacy 47–8
    isolation 46
    proximity 47
information technology (IT) 7, 47, 72–4,
    171, 172, 173
    atomization opportunities 173–5
        account-focused organizations
            174
        asset/service platforms 174
        product innovators 174
        system integrators 174
    innovation 79, 89–90, 99, 158–9
intellectual capital
    consumer experience 43
    economics of 41–3
    sharing 99
Interflora 104
Internet 37, 74, 114
Internet Service Providers (ISPs) 70
Internet Services Venture Vehicle
    (ISVV) 185
intimate computers 3

Java 174
joint ventures *see* partnerships

Kay, Alan 53
A.T. Kearney 33, 121

LevelSeas 167
Lucent 68, 69

McDonalds 85
McKinsey 33, 163
Mainspring 169
    atomization in telecoms sector 170
make-or-buy decisions 24
management 146–7
marketplace
    in atomic world 120–22
    horizontal 106–7, 125–6

fall and rise 118, 120
service platform 121, 153
vertical 11, 25–6, 35, 100, 106, 114, 125, 184, 185
communications channel 120
death 116–17
emergence 116
future 117–18
oil sector 165
webspinners as link 122
MCI-Worldcom 169
Mendeleev, Dimitri Ivanovich 124
mergers and acquisitions (M&A) 36, 37
failures 30–31
reasons for 28–30
successes 31
Merrill Lynch 107
Meyer, Chris 82
MG Rover 88
Microsoft 47, 73, 75, 76
Mobil 165
mobile networks 50–51, 53
third generation 58, 70
molecules 3, 4, 14, 113, 122
MP3 devices 51

Napster 48
National Center for Supercomputer Applications (NCSA) 76
NEC 68
Net Future Expectations (NFE) 64–5, 76
Net Future Opportunity (NFO) 65
Netscape 75, 76
newpowercompany.com 102
Nike 41
Nokia 86, 166
Nortel 68, 69
NTT 80

OceanConnect 167
oil sector *see* energy sector
Oracle 174
outsourcing 74, 109, 188

PA Consulting 33

Packard, David 175
Palm Pilot 51
partnerships
benefits
accelerate internal transformation 184
enhance external stakeholder perception 184
halo effect 192, 194
leveraging collective relationships 188
new 184
new business model 188–9
operation 189–92
mobilizing support 193
pay-off 193–4
prerequisite conditions 192–3
thoughts to commercialization 192
as shared incubator 189, 190, 192
shared services 185–6
asset broking 187
consultancies 187
e-customer care services 186
e-finance services 187
e-HR portals 186
e-knowledge in global trading 187
venture creation process 191
PATEX.com 89
PE-International 32
periodic table 124
personal computers 52–3
personal digital assistant (PDA) 50, 51
Plessey Electronics 68
politics 44–5
portfolio owners 11, 12, 98, 154, 202
atomization opportunities 161, 164
characteristics 109–10
PriceWaterhouseCoopers 33, 175
privatization 68
Procter & Gamble 42, 171, 172, 180
Psion Organiser 51

railroad investment 69–70
re-engineering 8–9, 31–2, 34, 36, 40, 73, 82, 187

fashion statement 31–2
real world issues 34
recession 73
Reflect.com 172, 180
regulation 124, 125
Regus 107–8
relational capital 7–8, 14, 71, 91–2,
    109, 184
  accelerated by trust 85–6
  complex interactions 82–3
  electronic markets 83–4
  increase value 79–82
  portals 84
  skills 148–9
  unlocking 95
  value 153, 154–6
Ringland, Gill 80
Royal Bank of Scotland 104

Sainsbury 88
Sapient 33
Scient 33
self-service 40–41
service platform 10, 13, 15, 98
  atomization opportunities 161, 163,
      171, 172, 174
  characteristics 106–7
  horizontal 121
    human relations 107
    office space 107
    procurement 106–7
  questions concerning 139
  strategy 176
shareholder wealth 146
  balanced view 64, 66
  cautious investment 63–4
  generation 75
  main factors
    innovative capacity 79, 89–90
    inter-business value networks 79,
        86–9
    stakeholder relationships 78,
        79–86
  net future expectations 64–5
  newly demanding community 77

telecommunications investment 71–2
  trust accelerates value 90–91
Shell 149, 151, 165, 166, 183
ShipChem 167
Siemens 68
smart company 13, 15, 90, 98, 172–3,
    199
  atomization opportunities 161, 163,
      166, 167, 169, 172, 174
  characteristics 98–9
  individual classification 203
  questions concerning 138–9
  strategy 168, 176
social agenda 39–40, 41
SRI International 33, 80
supplier-consumer relationship 40–41
suppliers 25, 40
supply chains 28, 36, 37, 70

taxation 123, 125
TCI 69
technology 38–9, 45, 48, 50, 187
  investment 59
telecommunications 58, 161,
    168–9
  atomization opportunities
    intelligent billing 171
    market-makers 170
    new service incubators 169
    service retailers 169
    shared networks 169–70
  investment 70–72
  railroad analogy 69–70
  revolution 68–9
Tesco 103, 104–5, 149, 161
Texaco 165
Trade Ranger 184
transaction costs 23–5, 95
  cheaper 36
  contract policing costs 24, 35
  discovery 24, 35
  engines 163–4
  internal 27–8, 35
  processing 163
  sourcing 24, 35

transfer pricing 125
Transora 171, 172
travel 43
Travelocity.com 43
trillenium 200
trust 8, 90–91, 100

Urwicks 32
US Postal Service 80

value networks 79
verbal communication 54
    digital cellular telephony 55
    speech recognition 55
    speech translation 55
Viant 33
virtual communication
    tele-entertainment 57
    tele-presence 57
    tele-robotics 57
    tele-surgery 57
    virtual conferencing 57
virtual reality (VR) techniques 57

visual communication 55–6
    desktop videoconferencing 56
    interactive TV 56
    multimedia kiosks 56

Wacker, Watts 80, 205
Wal-Mart 103, 161
water2water.com 101
weatherdesk.com 101
webspinner 12, 13, 98, 125, 138
    atomization opportunities 161, 163,
        166–7, 170
    characteristics 99–100
    individual classification 203
    link marketplaces 122
    questions concerning 138
    strategy 168, 176
Western Electric 68
World Wide Web 39, 43, 56, 75, 81,
        89–90

Yahoo! 75, 102–3, 149
Yet2Come.com 89